Bite the Writenausauros!
~
A Small Guide to Big Writing

Martha L Henning, Ph.D.

Kendall Hunt
publishing company

Cover design by Nan Curtis (2015)
Cover image © 2015 Shutterstock.com

Kendall Hunt
publishing company

www.kendallhunt.com
Send all inquiries to:
4050 Westmark Drive
Dubuque, IA 52004-1840

Copyright © 2015 by Martha L. Henning, Ph.D.

ISBN: 978-1-5249-3282-4

Kendall Hunt Publishing Company has the exclusive rights to reproduce this work, to prepare derivative works from this work, to publicly distribute this work, to publicly perform this work and to publicly display this work.

All rights reserved. No part of this publication may be reproduced, stored in a retrieval system, or transmitted, in any form or by any means, electronic, mechanical, photocopying, recording, or otherwise, without the prior written permission of the copyright owner.

Published in the United States of America

ACKNOWLEDGEMENTS

With gratitude to Dr. Gertrude Buck, first American woman Ph.D. of Rhetoric, for her inspiration and her brave challenge to the mechanization of teaching writing.

Thanks to Jim who fed me as I wrote and to my colleagues who encouraged me to create this text.

And, of course, in recognition of my family and three granddaughters in whose generation's use of language and diplomacy our future resides.

Cover art by Nan Curtis (2015)

Prologue

Turn of the century (1900) rhetorician, Dr. Gertrude Buck, confronted the prevailing notion of language as based in mechanics. She saw that language grows "organically" and "biologically" (her words) from an inner desire to communicate. Accordingly, she taught writing as a psychological process—beginning with a seed of thought, growing main trunks, then branching, leafing, and flowering into detail. Buck's process of writing thoughts and sentences works well with classical rhetorician, Cicero's, process of writing whole pieces of discourse. Cicero saw that discourse grows through a process of gathering information, arranging that information, voicing the now organized writing with attention to style, and finally, delivering the discourse in a strong and pleasing manner. This text works from the synergy of combining Buck and Cicero's processes of generating writing.

The monstrous Writenausauros was born of the mechanical age and grew up through the industrial age. Like language, the Writenausauros grew from the mechanization of creatures once naturally biologic. Alongside industrialization, the monster has entered into and grown to dominate whole aspects of culture, from business, law, and legislation to the local intimacies of individuals' minds. This book encourages writing students to bite the Writenausauros to bring language back to a more biologic and organic endeavor. Whereas texts that characterize language and writing as mechanical offer to fix broken writing, by characterizing language and writing as organic, this text offers to help students generate good effective writing in the first place.

Table of Contents

Introduction	1
Chapter I How to Write a Thought Thoughts and tips from Gertrude buck	9
Chapter II How to Write an Essay or A Road Trip with Cicero	25
Chapter III Invention or How to Gather Your Materials	39
Chapter IV Arrangement or How to Organize Your Materials	71
Chapter V Style or Don't Put Big Words In; Just Take the Little Ones Out	95
Chapter VI Memory or Keeping Your Head Together	149
Chapter VII Delivery or Unraveling the Mysteries of the MLA, APA, etc.	159
Chapter VIII Afterword ~ The Essay	171

INTRODUCTION

"Rhetoric" has come by its bad name by means of a historical slam. This guide aims to come to grips with that history. With a dab of history, you, too, can get comfortable thinking about rhetoric. Various reasons urge us to learn all we can from classical Greek and Roman rhetoricians. First, they knew what they were doing. They had the leisure (think slaves and women) to quiet their minds in order to ponder the nature of life and language—how life informs language and how language informs life. From these thinkers we can learn not only their thoughts, but also learn to value thinking, itself. You might try pulling the plug on your media some time to take a quiet walk and contemplate. Second, the thoughts of these Greek and Roman thinkers/rhetoricians have come through time to form the basis of our own language and thoughts. If you would like to gain some consciousness of your own life,[1] you would do well to look into the works of Plato, Aristotle, and others. Putting these factors together creates a powerful reason to look to classical rhetoricians and philosophers. They were really, really smart and their smarts form the basis of current social constructs of language that lurk in your head. Here you have not only the basis of your thought. The wisdom of the classical rhetoricians also forms the basis of thought of others around you. That is, you can learn to perceive how others think and might be attempting to influence you by heeding the wisdom of the ancients.

So hold on. Here we go!

---

[1] If, like Country Joe and the Fish in "Bass Strings," you want to "open up [your] head now just to see what [you] can find," you might ponder the thoughts of the ancient Greeks.

Old school rhetorician, Aristotle, explained that rhetoric is the obstetrician or midwife, delivering the baby that has gestated as someone's thought.[2] He also said that rhetoric is "the ability to see in any situation [<u>any</u>—really!], the available means of persuasion." Pretty powerful—maybe that's the basis for the old saying, "the pen is mightier than the sword." Maybe you could think of "rhetoric," as all the cool stuff that weaves in and out of language, making people think what and how they do. This guide offers to show, in part, how to do that weaving.

Bite the Writenausauros! draws its inspiration (steals?) from The Roman, Cicero, who held that rhetoric included a five step process: (1) strategies for figuring things out and (2) strategies for organizing one's thought. Style (3) had to do with word use; memory (4) put the composition into one's mind. Finally, delivery (5) gave students hints about body language. As a study, "rhetoric" lost much of its clout and respect with the big rise of science.[3] Some felt that the business of figuring things out and organizing materials was best left to the scientists and their scientific methods. Then with writing (and the printing press and internet and whatever is invented next week), we don't need to memorize anything anymore; we can just look things up. So with all this historical abuse, the sense of rhetoric as a study and guide for writing has been stripped of (1), (2), (3) – figuring, organizing, memorizing – and left with just two of Cicero's steps: style and delivery, amounting to song, dance, and presentation. Without the desire "to know," without science[4] and the desire to put substance into our memories, the American public is generally pretty happy attending

---

[2] OK, actually he said something like, "rhetoric is the handmaiden of dialectic"—except he said that in Greek.
[3] "Science": from the Latin word "scire" – to know.
[4] Even more depressingly, Chris Mooney and Sheril Kirshenbaum's *Unscientific America. How Scientific Illiteracy Threatens Our Future* shows how politics and the media have turned the American public against science. "Just 13 percent of the public now claims to follow science and technology" very closely. Nicholas Carr's *The Shallows. What the Internet is Doing to Our Brains* helps explain our cravings of flashy style and delivery.

to the shiny, flashy residue found on TV, in pop-ups, and amid the tantalizing magazine photos of grocery check-out lanes. That is, centuries of acculturation have had their way with you. Historically, you're perfectly justified in your grumpy aversion to a textbook offering tips from rhetoric study.

Well after the rise of science, back in the 1800s, the situation regarding the nature of "rhetoric" appeared somewhat as a toss-up. Some people still considered rhetoric as a study of human endeavors, thought, behavior, communication, and relationships. Other people considered learning grammar rules and tricks of speech or writing as the ticket for appearing more "high class" and so moving in appearances from "rough" farm workers to more smooth-talking town-folk. As more and more students began to see rhetoric studies as a means of economic or class self-betterment rather than a subject of philosophical-theological-psychological pondering, this latter sense of rhetoric began to die. At the turn of the century (the turn from 1800 to 1900, that is) with the mechanization of just about everything else, rhetoric largely went from a study of *how* people think to a study of the words themselves: the "mechanics" of language.

Now in the twenty-first century, the popular sense of the word, "rhetoric" has almost come to refer to techniques for lying effectively; the media steams with reports of "rhetoric" oozing from lawyers, politicians, and shady finance people whose very language turns them into caricatures and stereotypes of cagey, suspicious characters. To which the early Greek philosopher Plato would say, "I told you so!" As long ago as around 400-375 BCE (explanation below), Plato warned that teaching and learning principles of language could turn the arts of expression and communication into a cookbook-style of discourse—five parts emotion, one part logic, and stir. He feared the study of rhetoric could provide recipes for ignorant speakers to persuade unsuspecting voters that what *seems* true *is* true and so persuade those voters to act accordingly and thus create very real (and bad) situations based on perceptions of the unreal. If that's not enough reason to drop the whole business, occasionally someone armed with a knowledge of how to use persuasive language adds greedy self-interest to ignorance and bulldozers right over the interests of others—scary. Or even worse, some entity armed with sufficient funding to buy the media rights to your and everyone else's minds hires someone armed with a knowledge of how to use persuasive language—potentially deadly.

For Old School Readers

That "BCE" back there means "Before Common Era," currently side-stepping religious references such as "BC," "Before Christ." Similarly, AD ("Anno Domini") (in the year of our/the Lord) is now "CE" for "Common Era." Using "CE" also side-steps using "*vulgaris aerae*" or "Vulgar Era," which some might find quite appropriate for about now. And Istanbul (Not Constantinople):
http://www.youtube.com/watch?v=dsRuurcTTSk

INTERLUDE

- Go into "your world" of family, work, friends, etc. and ask at least three people what they think "rhetoric" means. Try to make some sense of their answers; where did their ideas or bewilderment come from?
- Some people think rhetoric refers to ways to use language
    - to beat people up
    - to communicate
    - to discover new truths
    - to get one's own way
    - to express oneself—regardless of who's listening/reading—that is, to rant.

Add these possibilities to the possibilities you got from asking people about rhetoric.

Then find in a newspaper or a magazine some examples of these uses of language.

Given the current state of affairs (and affairs of state), then, courses in writing and thinking about argument and critical thought would do well to alert students to some strategies of self-defense. Further, a study of making one's way through life in terms of language might also do well to tap directly into some of the original sources of thinking about the ins and outs of language—sources that show how you might better use language while at the same time provide you with some means of perception of how language uses you. And so to survive and (hopefully) to flourish, swimming in the ever-self-revising element of culture called "language," through a study of rhetoric, we can move closer to some foundations of the culture's (and so often our own) thoughts and utterances.

Various aspects of rhetoric theory have wriggled through time and space[5] to form various of the cultural assumptions and habits that are in our heads. No matter how much you consider yourself an individual liberated from culture, the general way of *how* you think (as opposed to, but maybe including some of *what* you think) infiltrates your head vis-à-vis your culture. By getting to know how you think and communicate, you can begin to control your own culturally induced habits. Once you take a look at how your own habits for thinking and communicating have come to you, you can begin to play with how your head works. You can add new ways of thinking, speaking, arguing, writing; rearrange old ways of thinking, speaking,

---

[5] This idea—thought and language habits wriggling through time and places—has a trendy word for you to use: "diachronic." Very impressive. The "dia" part means "back and forth" or "from point to point"; the "chronic" part means through time. Put those together and you have ideas moving back and forth through time. Use the term like: "This concept evolves diachronically . . . blah, blah." If you want to stop all the time wriggling to consider how various thought and language habits appear at just one particular time, you can use the term, "synchronic."

arguing, writing; have more tools in your cerebral toolbox; and, maybe most importantly, feel in control of choosing and using your own cerebral tools to think, speak, argue, and write.

THIS BOOK

In the past few decades, lovers of language, reacting to the common meaning of rhetoric as something bad, and feeling the loss of rhetoric's wealth of ideas for thinking about language, began to go back to study the philosophical, psychological, communication type of rhetoric. Unfortunately, much of that study became voiced in a mysterious, difficult, academic language about language. Granted, language about language does get pretty abstract at times. BUT, the study of rhetoric can be very useful and fairly entertaining for people who by some turn of fate encounter the subject.

Bite the Writenausauros! challenges the stereotype that a study of rhetoric has to be about mechanized, ivory tower, rule-bound and gagged, stifling, up-tight language. Learning about rhetoric as an art will give you alternative ways to deal with your sense of self and life. As a listener/reader, you will learn some hidden ways that language can trip you up or mess with your mind. As a speaker/writer, you will learn pointers for perceiving and communicating with strength, grace, and clarity.

© mariait/Shutterstock.com

I
HOW TO WRITE A THOUGHT
THOUGHTS AND TIPS FROM GERTRUDE BUCK

© alex74/Shutterstock.com

By 1900, the industrial revolution was in full force. Industrialists were building factories and fortunes while vast numbers of citizens worked in those factories, often for very little in the way of wages. The language of the day reflected and perpetuated these economic and social movements. It became just as important to associate subjects or circumstances with the word "science" (or "mechanics") as it is today to associate subjects or circumstances with the word "technology."

People of that era spoke and wrote of the science of religion, the science of health, the science of language, the science of you-name-it, just as we currently speak and write of the technology of health, communications, etc.[1] As time moved from the nineteenth to the twentieth century, language and rhetoric studies gradually lost their sense of enriching the student and gained more of a sense of enriching pockets. The study of grammar as a way of knowing gave way to a study of grammar as rule-bound. Eventually, the culture's love affair with industry, science, and rules became so prevalent that grammar increasingly looked like and came to be called "mechanics." The mode, "Argumentation," became a war-like exercise in which one person or team tried to "beat" or subdue an opposing side. Generally, people came to value rhetoric and language studies not as a means to living a more psychologically and intellectually rewarding life, but as a means of beating one's way to the economic or social top in a dog-eat-dog, competitive, social Darwinist vision of the world. So much for enlightenment.

---

[1] For example my Dilbert-style cubicle is in the Communications Technology (CT) building where people engage with such "technologies" as literature, writing, languages, sculpture, painting, and dance.

Dr. Gertrude Buck

(With the kind permission of Vassar College)

Enter an important exception: America's first woman Ph.D. of Rhetoric, Dr. Gertrude Buck. Buck challenged her time's developing industrial and mechanical paradigms as they threatened to bulldoze the human spirit. Writing at the turn of the last century, Buck gives us several things to think about even more than a century later.

From her we can think of

- argumentation not as "war," but as "friendly persuasion";
- grammar and such stylistic devices not as "mechanics," but as "organic" urges to communicate with one another;
- learning to speak and write not as hoops to jump through, but as growing from students' desire to involve themselves in making meaning;
- literature not as an object of art or window to culture, but as an activity to engage in
- communication as a communal activity, in which participants work together to gain some sense of "truth";
- education not as learning in various unconnected fields—math, history, grammar, art, etc.—but a "systematic instruction" of "organized, interrelated, and interdependent knowledge."[2]

Buck would have students write well to enable them to learn more richly in the arts and sciences. In like manner, she would have students learn in the arts and sciences to enable them to write more richly.

---

[2] Several colleges currently offer such a conceptually integrated curriculum and pedagogy, for example, Hampshire College, MA and The Evergreen State College, WA.

THINKING

Buck also gives us some handy tips regarding how we go about thinking. Ways of thinking have changed through the ages. Generally, the deductive method—drawing specifics from the general or from the abstract—has been associated with the "dark" ages, women's cognitive history, and the imagination. The inductive method —seeking cold facts as foundation for drawing generalizations and abstractions—has been associated with the "enlightenment," men's cognitive history, and the scientific method. Heeding Buck while enjoying our place in time, we can now draw on both of these ways of thinking without placing some value or privilege of the one over the other. Buck suggests utilizing the best of both systems of thought as a way of getting us out of what she saw as a "muddle of criticism." We can take her idea further as we consider "all the world a stage" and so not approach phenomena as the aggressive judge and critic, but as the friendly and inquisitive judge and critic. Buck would have us in our thinking and reading and writing, develop social standards which deepen aesthetics and extend morality. As she advocates "Art for Life's Sake," perhaps now we can begin as well to appreciate "Life for Art's Sake." That is, we might begin to consider discourse as a gift we can generate through our daily lives as well as considering our lives as a product of our discourse.

Taking from Buck the view of language as organic, evolving, social voices, we can only hope to respect, use, generate, and enjoy language to enrich not only ourselves, but also to enrich our culturally evolving world.

And now for a historical interlude.

Godey's Lady's Book

November, 1858
Volume 57, page 463

Editors' Table.

WHO ARE THE AUTHORS OF THE ATLANTIC TELEGRAPH

In a late number of *Fraser's Magazine*, there appeared an able and interesting article written by Mr. Henry Thomas Buckle, in which he describes "The Influence of Woman on the Progress of Knowledge." The summary of the writer's views may be stated thus: -----

"Our knowledge is composed not of facts, but of the relations which facts and ideas bear to themselves and to each other; and real knowledge consists not in an acquaintance with facts, which only makes a pedant, but in the use of facts, which makes a philosopher.

"The scientific inquirer, properly so called, that is, he whose object is merely truth, has only two ways of attaining his result. He may proceed from the external world to the internal; or he may begin with the internal, and proceed to the external. In the former case, he studies the facts, presented to his senses, in order to arrive at a true idea of them; in the latter case, he studies the ideas already in his mind, in order to explain the facts of which his senses are cognizant. If he begin with the facts, his method is inductive; if he begin with ideas, it is deductive.

"The inductive philosopher collects phenomena either by observation or by experiment, and from them rises to the general principle or law which explains and covers them. The deductive philosopher draws the principle from ideas already existing in his mind, and explains the phenomena by descending on them, instead of rising from them."

After explaining and illustrating these general principles in various ways, the author proceeds to establish two propositions: "First, That women naturally prefer the deductive method to the inductive. Secondly, That woman, by encouraging in men deductive habits of thought, have rendered an immense, though unconscious, service to the progress of knowledge, by preventing scientific investigators from being as exclusively inductive as they would otherwise be.

"In regard to women being by nature more deductive, and men more inductive, you will remember that induction assigns the first place to particular facts; deduction to general propositions or ideas. Now, there are several reasons why women prefer the deductive, and if I may so say, ideal method. They are more emotional, more enthusiastic, and more imaginative than men; they therefore live more in an ideal world; while men, with their colder, harder, and austere organizations, are more practical and more under the dominion of facts, to which they consequently ascribe a higher importance.   - - -

It is not true that the greatest modern discoveries have all been made by induction; and the circumstance of its being believed to be true is one of many proofs how much more successful Englishmen have been in making discoveries than in investigating the principles according to which discoveries are made.

WRITING

Buck offers some valuable and timely tips for turning around what has come to us as some dysfunctional ways of teaching and learning to write. Somewhere in time in the mid-twentieth century, writing teachers saw their function as that of the literary critic. A student wrote something, and, like a good critic, the teacher "corrected" and/or "graded" it. This way of doing things brought with it quite a few assumptions. First, the student was considered small whereas the teacher was considered big. That is, the classroom was a "teacher-centered" place where the teacher had authority and held the answers. This set-up, in turn, meant that there were, in fact, answers or situations in learning of right or wrong to which a teacher could hold a key. In writing classes, then, the teacher with the literary-critical mind-set wrote with authority relative to the "correctness" of student writing. Grammar was not seen as social conventions growing out of eons of time and space and peoples, but was seen as "good" or "bad." Buck helps us out of this bind. With Buck's tips in mind, we can now consider and use those grammatical structures that best promote communication. Most American colleges prefer the social convention of Standard English—and there definitely are rights and wrongs *within* that dialect. The New York police force prefers to communicate the social convention of a dialect comprising various acronyms, street slang, and legalese,[3] a dialect in which there are definite rights and wrongs even as it evolves. Perhaps we can take a tip from Buck and speak not of good and bad language, but of language appropriate or not appropriate to its particular situation—with that situation dependent on a balance among the conventions of the community in which you are writing, your purpose, your audience, and your message itself. In1897, in the face of all things mechanical, while institutions of higher learning were having a love affair with science, Gertrude Buck actually proclaimed the "organic" nature of language.[4]

---

[3] See Marcus Laffey, "The Word on the Street," *The New Yorker*, 10 Aug. 98, page 36.
[4] "Indeed, everything comes alive when contradictions accumulate." ~~ Gaston Bachelard. *The Poetics of Space*. (translated, 1964).

In a biological manner, our thoughts begin with a seed: "damn," "whoa," "Dude," "hey," "ouch." From the seed of thought then grows the main trunks of our thought. Using Buck's example, the "ouch" can grow into the sentence with the main branches: "Ouch! I cut myself."

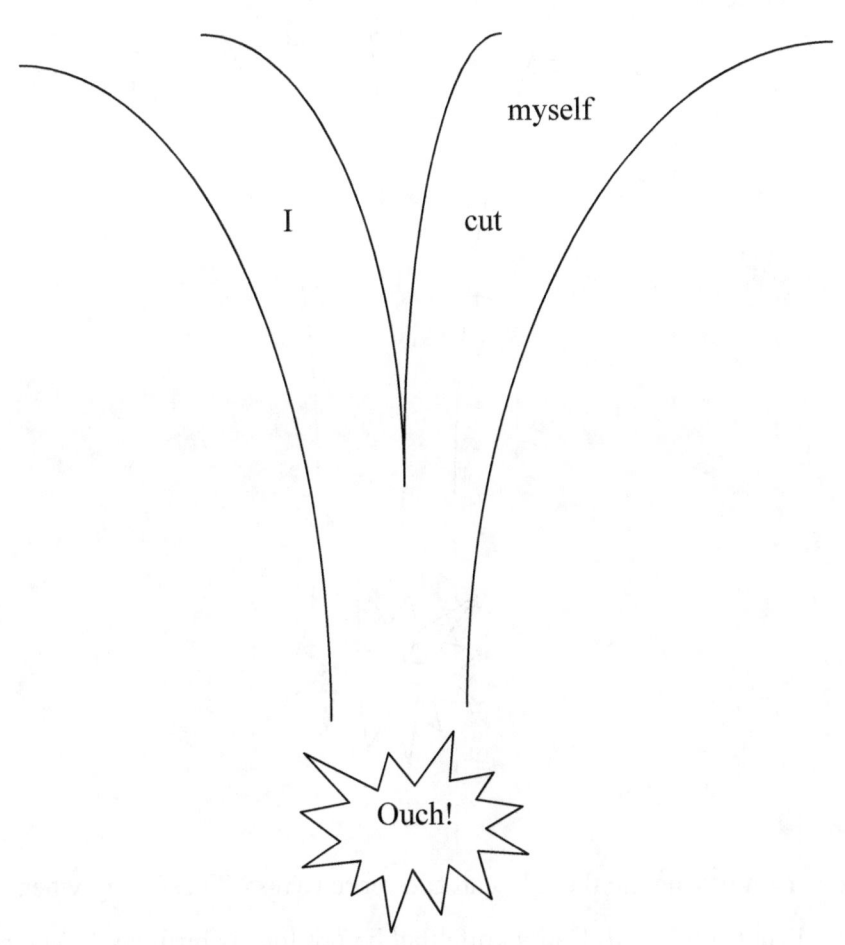

The thought then grows in the mind:

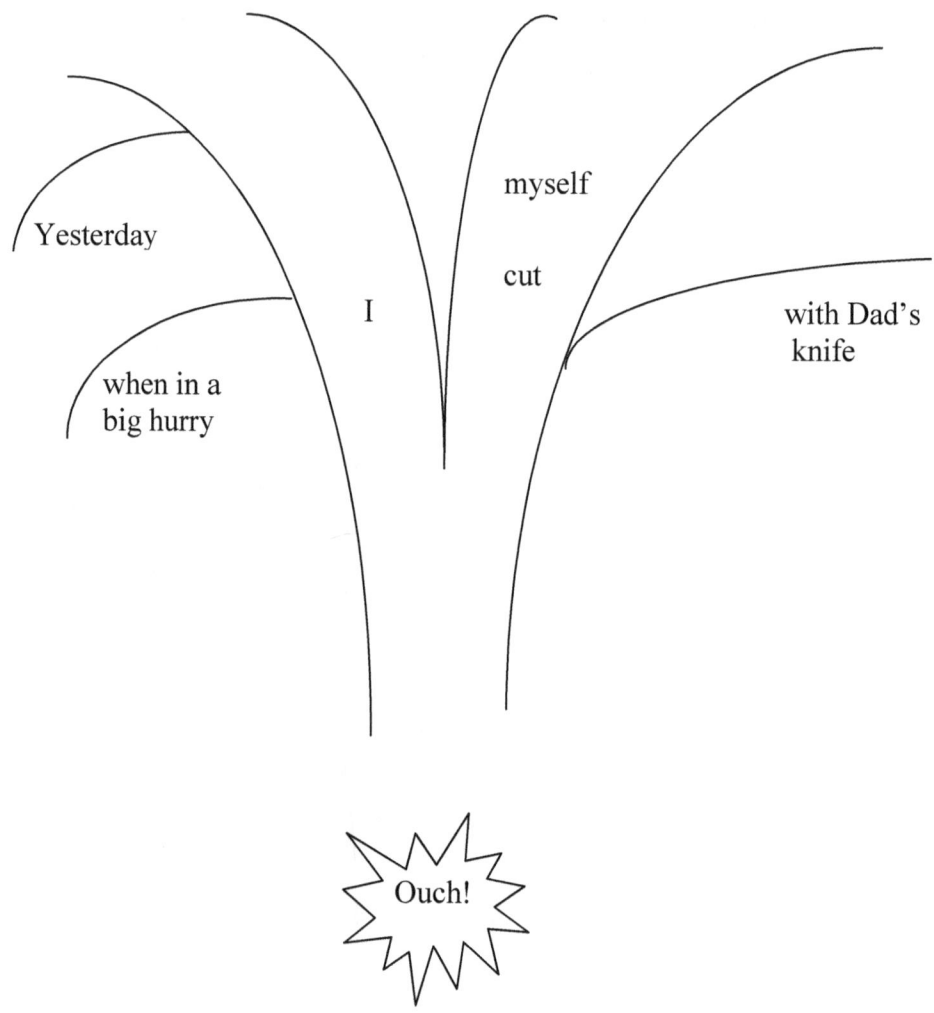

The person having the thought can add more twigs: "Yesterday when in a big hurry I cut myself with Dad's knife that he got for his birthday." Maybe another seed will grow from a flower and form its own new sentence: "Dad hates birthdays."

Buck's conception of language development encourages the clear thinking and writing that you will encounter, in "Chapter V, Style." If you can put the subject that grows in your mind into the grammatical subject place, then you won't have to edit out all the silly stuff: "~~It can be seen that~~ I cut myself." Actually, if elementary teachers were to teach writing using Buck's tips for developing thoughts and sentences, high school teachers would not have to teach students to edit out peripheral filler. Everyone would write in good strong, clear, dynamic language.[5]

Here are some places where you can try out Buck's method. First plant the seed of your thought. From this seed then grow the subject and verb. Then grow some "foliage." Of course this method is almost insultingly simple, but consider all the time that you'll save editing if you can train your writing mind to avoid all the useless junk that gets edited out later. Here you go~~

---

[5] Tell that to the lawyers who make their living by obfuscating communication.

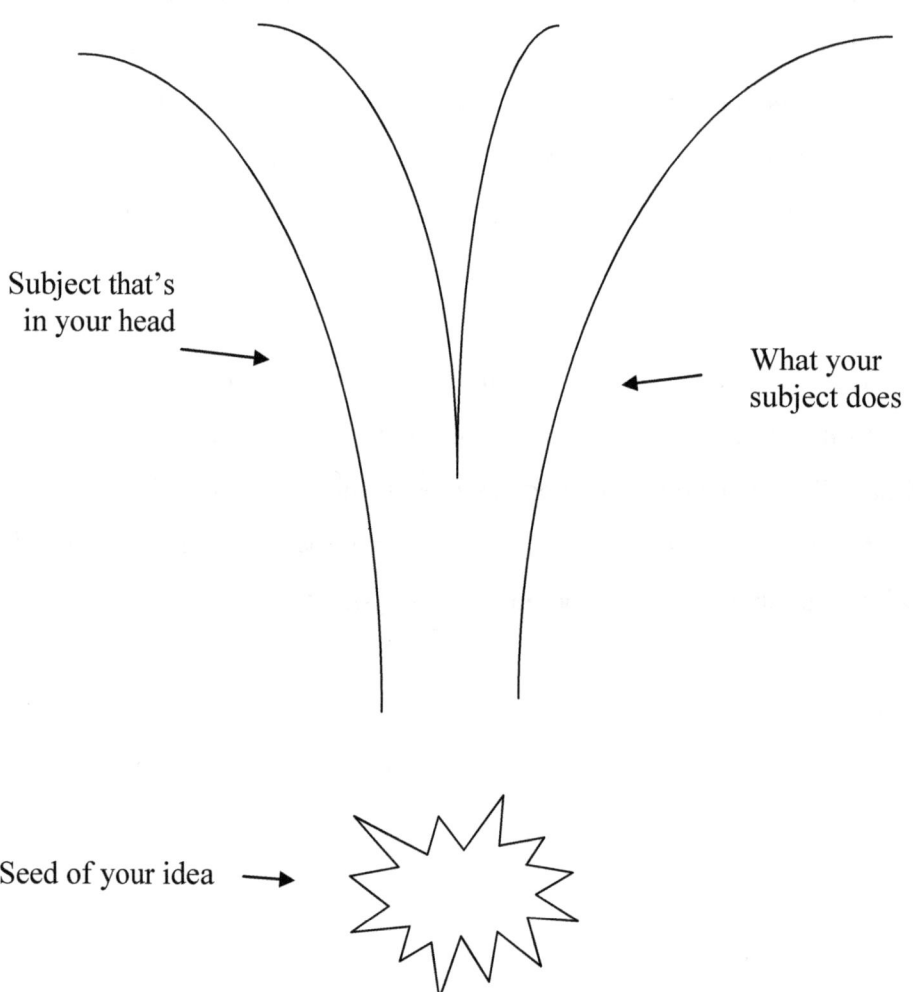

Now add some "foliage," twigs and leaves:

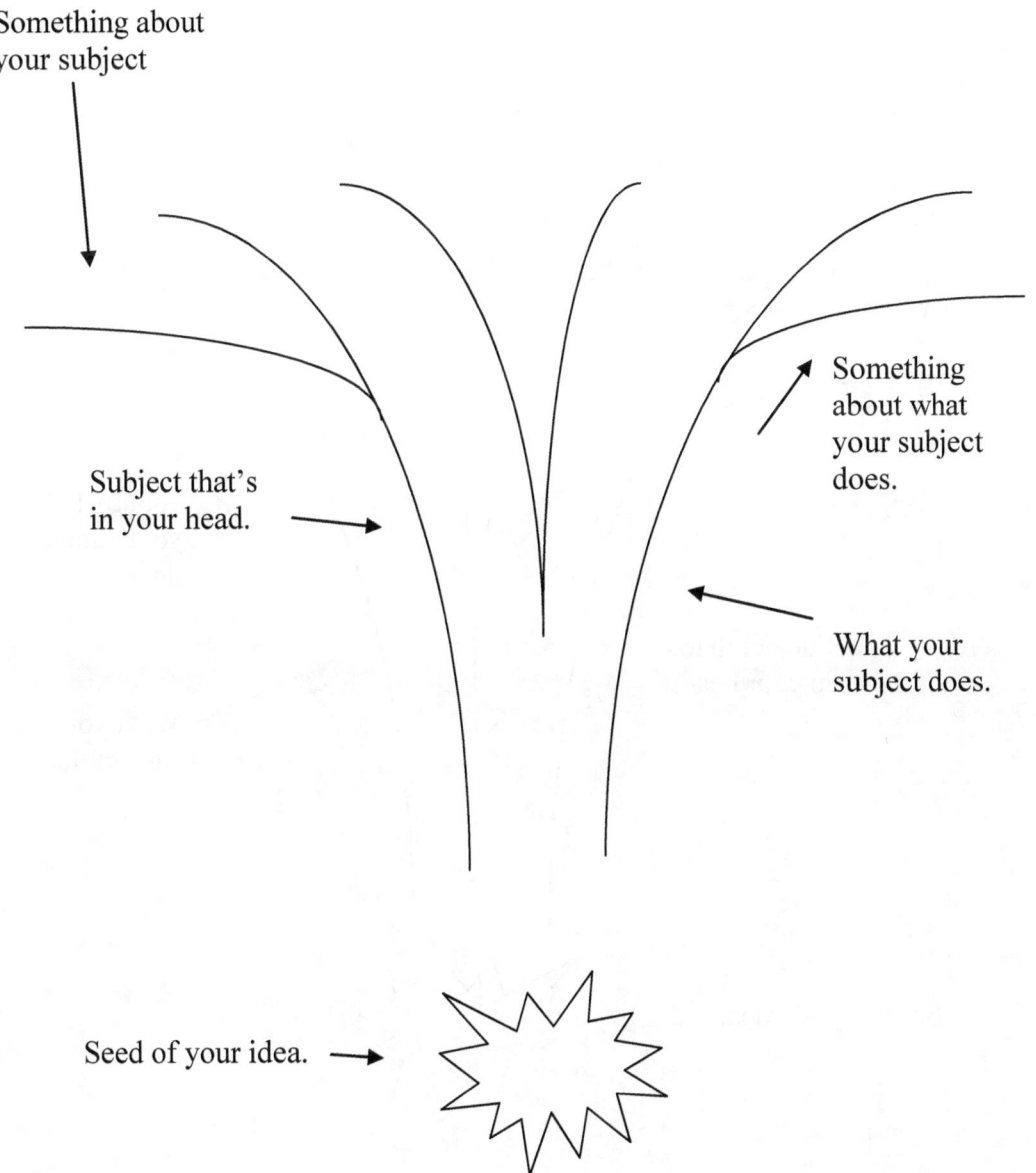

Now add as much "foliage" as you'd like. Draw your own additional lines. Have fun!

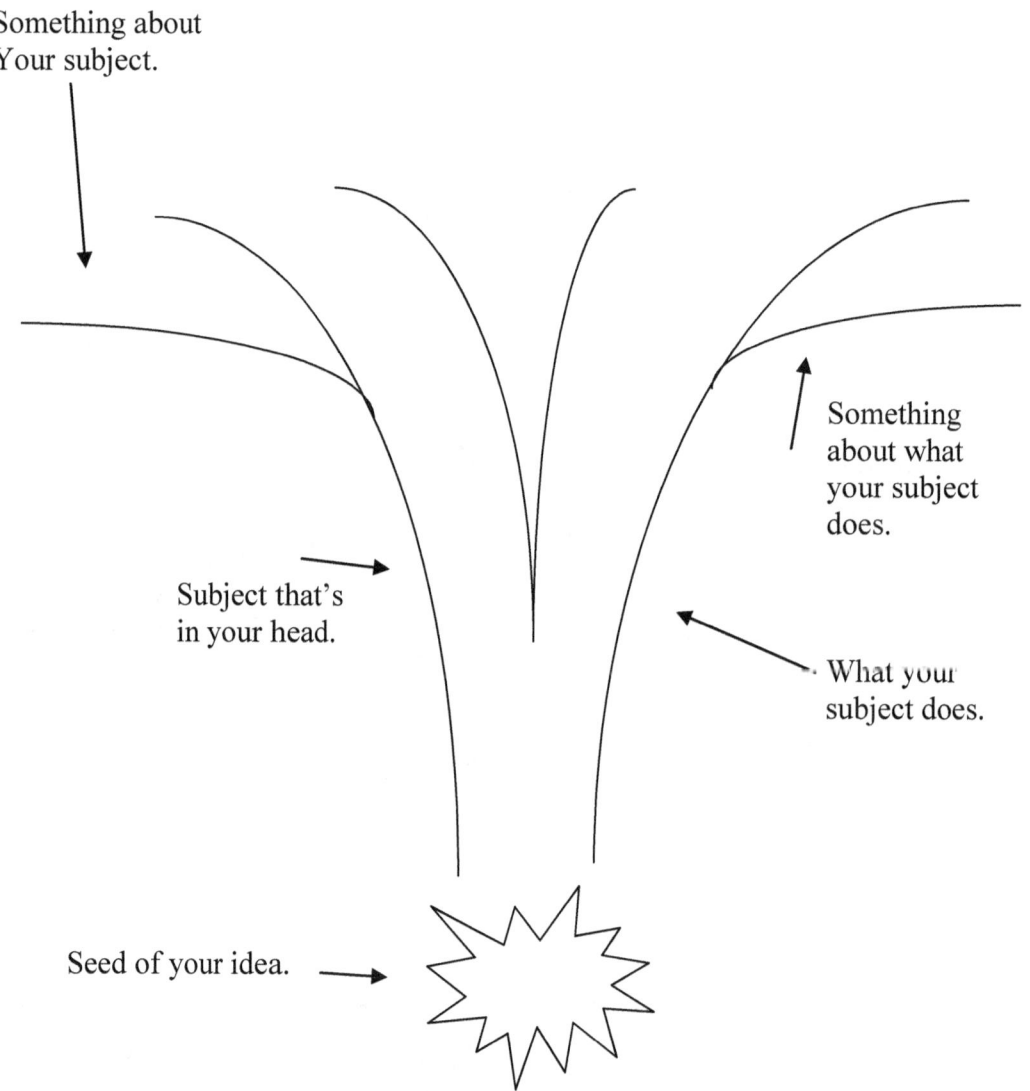

Later (1916) Buck applies this observation of the genesis of language to the larger field of literary criticism. She sees that when language comes to the listener or reader, it literally sows and transplants and grows thoughts in the mind of that listener/reader. As Buck says, "literature is, then, the final flowering in a creative literary act." What we can gather, then, is that we do not necessarily have to be defensive when reading; we do not necessarily need to be thinking of the next "zinger" when someone else is speaking. Instead, we can (as advocated by the Vietnamese Zen Buddhist monk, teacher, author, speaker) Thich Nhat Hanh,[6] work to listen with compassion and speak deliberatively.

Finally, in speaking of an "organic curriculum," Buck shows that children (and, by extension, college writing students) can learn to write with "greater thoroughness" in an "organic system" in which subjects are not imposed onto the student from the outside. Rather, the student can learn to write with "greater thoroughness" when naturally developing his or her own interests. A student cannot forget issues of concern when at school. The student who has the opportunity to express his or her own concerns as subjects through which to practice writing skills "owns" his or her writing. In the act of the natural development of personal interests, the writing "is in a real literal sense, his own self." And, at the end of the writing course when students leave for "the wide, wide world," [7] and instructors sigh and wonder whatever will become of them, those students will more than likely not find assignments to write about.

---

[6] Interestingly, in Berkeley, California, September 13, 2001.
[7] The title of America's first million-selling (non-serialized) novel, by Susan Warner, 1850.

Rather, those writing students will (hopefully) someday feel the desire, from the inside ⇨ out, to write to an editor, to a state legislator, to a grandparent, to a lover – or combinations of people who comprise a wide audience.

© alex74/Shutterstock.com

Your author hopes that readers can use the tips offered in this text to communicate clearly and in the tradition of rhetoricians who have considered language a gift to promote both the personal and social good.

Listen, read, and write well!

II

How to Write an Essay

or

A Road Trip with Cicero

"Cicero adds method to the madness."

—Diane Moylan[1]

© Alessandro/Shutterstock.com

We now move to the last gasps of the Roman Republic and subsequent beginnings of the Roman Empire. As a young man schooled in the tradition of the Greek rhetoricians, Cicero learned to uphold the idea that men should act in the best interests of the community. He lived at an interesting time—when such views were challenged by men who thought the most powerful should take over. Shortly after the assassination of Julius Caesar, Cicero, in 43 BCE, was beheaded.[2] Born in 106 BCE, Marcus Tullius Cicero,[3] comes to us not only as a writer, teacher, speaker, and supporter of the Republic, but also as a student.

---

[1] Student final exam: 1 June 1995.
[2] I'll spare you the very gory details.
[3] Oh, go ahead; you can call him "Tully."

By the time Cicero was a teenager, education for young men of his (rather privileged) class to a good extent focused on training in rhetoric. Anyone who wanted to develop into a well spoken person needed to know just about everything else there was to know in the world in order to use that knowledge to think and speak. So young men like Cicero worked to gather into themselves the riches of wide reading, especially in philosophy, law, and history. They also worked to internalize rhetorical skills—like using humor, building one's own argument, squashing an opposing argument, and psychologically controlling an audience.

Like others from boy to youthish—15 to 20 or so—Cicero found himself trying to figure out all of Greek and Roman rhetoric—tons and tons of complex stuff. Given that the study of rhetoric encompassed all there was to know in life (in order to have wisdom and something to say about everything), scholars for a century or two had busied themselves to schematize, systematize, organize all existing knowledge—including all knowledge of rhetoric. So as Cicero learned this systematized version of rhetoric studies, he wrote something that we call *De Inventione*. But, evidently, he didn't mean to. As you'll see, "invention" is only a piece of what the writing was supposed to discuss. The real name of Cicero's early work should have been *Rhetorici Libri.* Even worse, later on in life, Cicero hints that publishing the thing was some sort of accident or mistake.[4] As notes he took[5] from his teacher, Molon, and adapted to Latin, the piece shows us <u>how</u> Roman students learned rhetoric.

---

[4] Later on in life, Cicero wrote:
> The incomplete work—merely a rough draft—which escaped from my note-books between boyhood and youth is hardly worthy of my age and the experience that I have acquired from the many important cases in which I have appeared.

(From the introduction by H.M. Hubbell, page vii, in the little red book of the Loeb Classical Library, Cicero's *De Inventione*.)

[5] Keep track of your class notes lest twenty years from now after you've become wildly famous, someone publishes them.

Importantly, the value of *De Inventione* for post-industrial twenty-first-century students isn't so much in its material, but in its method. Although Cicero himself knew and thought in the language and the sense of the Greek philosophers, with his *De Inventione*, rhetoric loses some of its philosophical richness and becomes more utilitarian and pragmatic. Apparently, when faced with teaching the art, discipline, science, theory, and practice of rhetoric, Roman teachers focused on some method they could give students to get them through the complexities of it all. Cicero's notes move from Aristotle's study of what rhetoric **is,** to a study of **how** to develop discourse – how to write. Cicero shows us how by giving us five steps[6]—namely: **invention, arrangement, style, memory,** and **delivery.**

---

[6] That *De Inventione* turns this study of rhetoric and writing to a step program seems quite handy and apropos for our current culture whose people increasingly turn to such step programs and instruction books "for dummies."

HOW TO WRITE
CICERO: ANALOGY OF THE ROAD TRIP

Writing, Ciceronian method, happens somewhat like a road trip.

Your Subject.

First, you sit around, maybe with friends or colleagues, and figure out the general direction of where you want to go. This is called settling on a topic[7] or subject.

Invention.

Next comes what Cicero called *invention*.[8] Take a few days to gather up supplies.[9] Several approaches here. If you bake your own cookies, make your own

---

[7] Through translations and time, the Greek idea of "topoi" and our own concept of "topic" have taken on quite different meanings. The Greek, "topoi" refers to "places to go" in the sense of what you do with a subject to get more material by checking out such "places" as cause & effect or moving from the piece to the whole, etc. Our current sense of "topic" refers to a subject itself. We have other words also relating to place, like topographic or topography. Consider the residual metaphors that cross these time boundaries: "Where do you want to go with this topic?"

[8] Well, sort of. Actually the meaning for the Latin *inventio* has been about as skewed as the obscurely related meaning for duct tape. The currently abused substance, duct tape, was once used to tape heating ducts— "duct" from the Latin, "ducio" meaning "to lead"—like The Duke of Earl. Now we use duct tape to fix and create all sorts of things. With an oddly similar mindset, by sticking letters in and on the end of *invenio,* we have come up with "invention," which implies that we can make something. The Latin sense of *invenio*, however, comes from the Latin *venio*, meaning "to come" and giving us the word, "vent," which we fix with duct tape. The more proper sense of what Cicero means by *invenio* means "to come in on" or so "to find," something that exists already and you have to struggle to find it; you can't just make it up.

[9] The Romans called the gathered supplies for making discourse (here, writing) "copiae." Their idea of supplies gathered for discourse related to their idea of supplies gathered for

tabouli, juice your own carrots, etc. and pack your own cooler, you know exactly what you have. That's like getting *primary sources* for your writing. To get primary sources for writing, go interview people, find original letters and manuscripts in the archives of big libraries, visit old battlegrounds, create the gooey, succulent mid-night snack that gorgeous Porphyro brings to sensual-dreaming enchanted Madeline in Keats's "The Eve of St. Agnes." Going to original sources is considered very scholarly and can lead to too much fun when you start going further and further — like juicing the carrots, baking the cookies, adding little slices of ginger and beets and maple syrup. That is, primary research/packing your own cooler can draw you into whole new worlds, which may reveal wonderful discoveries, but you could get so involved in the preparation that you totally forget about going on the road-trip or writing the paper—until someone taps you on the shoulder that you've run out of time.

    On the other hand, if you pack your cooler with packaged foods, courtesy of the foods industry, that's like getting *secondary sources* for your writing. To get secondary sources for writing, go get books in which various authors tell you about their interviews, give you their ideas about original sources, describe historical situations (from their perspectives), or slam some author as fat and writing flowery stuff (Poe on women authors). The academic community views using such secondary sources as just fine as long as you tell your readers where you got your materials. You need to cite your sources as you write and then put the whole citation on a Works Cited page at the end of your essay. Listing the whole citations (in alphabetical order) is sort of like food packagers having to list their ingredients somewhere on their labels. Using lots of sources of any kind makes you look knowledgeable and

---

war—wagon-loads of ammunition and food and clothes and sleeping bags—that is, the supplies for a road-trip plus weaponry.

well-read.[10] Just remember that using secondary sources puts you in partnership with those writers whose ideas you use. You might try to find out what current academic folks think of your sources. Like, currently, some feminist professors might not think much of you using Freudian explanations or references to certain critics. So you can follow historic dialogues in which one scholar says something about something and then another scholar "corrects" the first, and a third "corrects" the second, and so on.

  Finally, if working in all out efficiency mode, you can go for the gold-mines of fast pre-packaged coolers and information. Just as Aunt Tudy (she's in Nebraska) fills the cooler with all sorts of goodies for you, as a writer, you can go get a bibliography of some subject. That is, you might be able to find a book that lists practically all the articles and books about a subject. And then there are bibliographies of these bibliographies.

The internet offers lists of sources already put together for you. For example, you can use Wikipedia, not for what an entry reveals about your subject, but for its gold mine of sources—where those writers got their materials. Just keep in mind that using someone else's research can color your ideas to look like theirs; like when Aunt Tudy packed the cooler with blueberry yogurt, grape sodas, blue corn chips, and her famous purple potato salad.

So now you have piles of supplies all packed up. Note that the nature of your supplies will, in part, determine the nature of your road-trip and/or writing. If you take off without adequate supplies—planning to rely on dumpster-expertise on the one hand or to flashing plastic on the other hand—you may have difficulty and/or have to pay later.

---

[10] The Greeks called this sense of the writer's credibility, "ethos."

Arrangement.

With the Subaru wagon ready to roll and a general direction in mind, you now face the wheels on the car that make contact with the road. Where, exactly, do you want to go? When "on the road again" (Willy), you pull out the map that someone has failed to fold properly, and start hashing out an itinerary.[11] In a car full of folks, you will have to collaborate and come to some consensus of what route will be the most effective, prudent, enjoyable, scenic, and/or fast for those who will experience the road trip. With writing, you will need to map your ideas so that they will reach your reader in an effective, prudent, enjoyable, scenic, and/or fast manner, that is, depending on *the needs and expectations of your generic academic reader*. Like others,[12] Cicero speaks of *positioning* ideas in discourse. Some books and teachers call this reckoning process, "arrangement." Spending time and energy figuring out where you plan to go in your road-trip and/or paper may well be the most important factor in determining the outcome.[13] Figure out a plan and write it down and follow it so that you won't crash when you come to an intersection of fast-moving vehicles and/or thoughts. Naturally, where you plan to go in your road-trip/writing will have something to do with your supplies and vice-versa. And, naturally, where you plan to go will have something to do with what happens along the way in geography and language. Plan well lest you get lost—lose your passengers and/or readers.

---

[11] "Way to go," in geographical sense—but not topoi—rather than in the congratulatory sense.

[12] In one of his several little plays or dialogues, Plato shows us that unplanned writing looks like "swimming upstream (on your back) through the current of your own discourse." Not pretty.

[13] This bears repeating: spending time and energy figuring out where you plan to go in your road-trip and/or paper may well be the most important factor in determining the outcome.

Style.

With trip underway, you proceed along your planned route, using your supplies as needed, working them into the experience of the journey. When writing, you similarly embed the materials you have gathered into the arrangement you have developed. You put your ideas where they belong according to your plan. And you do that with language. Don't stop and go, getting hung-up on the phantoms that attach themselves to words or you might crash or your writing might come to a roadblock called writer's block. A famous writing teacher, Peter Elbow, says to turn off the computer screen so you won't go nuts trying to find the "right" word of so many words out there, and forget where you meant to go.[14] Remember where you mean to go and just put your vehicle on cruise control and get your ideas and miles behind you. You can think about the little details later. Wanting to explore every little pebble along the road, you won't get anywhere fast. Wanting to explore every little word in your own discourse, you won't get anywhere fast.[15]

---

[14] Elbow gave this advice before the popularity of laptops without detachable monitors.

[15] Actually, exploring every little pebble along the way in a road-trip might make more sense than exploring every little word in writing because in a road-trip, "we may never pass this way again" (Seals and Crofts). Writing departs from the linear nature of the road-trip. Writing is no longer embedded in stone while you're doing it; rather, a writer continuously makes writing "happen." That is, writing happens as a process like some "recursive virus." You can return to the ideas and to the words that hold and create those ideas and even to the empty route/ arrangement plan. You can return to all aspects of your own writing and you can invite others to comment on the various aspects and the various states of how/where that recursive virus happens to be growing at various times. Don't get hung up on words because you can go back and ~~fix~~ them, ~~switch~~ them, ~~replace~~ them, ~~reword~~ them, ~~get rid of~~ them, make them just how you want them.

Memory.

In the old days, students put their own language (speeches, essays) into their memories to show off to their fathers or anyone else who cared to listen. Rather than diminish our faculty of memory as you will see our culture would have us do, we can expand on the ancient sense of memory as a firm mental grasp on ideas and words.

As you travel, remember where you've gone and where you are, and where you plan to go. In writing, remember all that and be sure to remember your reader. Remember that your reader is not you. Your reader does not remember all that you remember. You may remember what you learned growing up in Kentucky, but your academic reader may have grown up in New Jersey. Writing for someone whose head is filled with stuff that is totally different from the stuff in your head poses difficulties. It gets worse. You have to get concepts from your head to the head of someone else who has no clue what's in your head and do all that not with the concepts at all, but in some weird code of little funny marks called letters. And the little funny marks don't look much at all like the concepts you want to give someone else.[16]

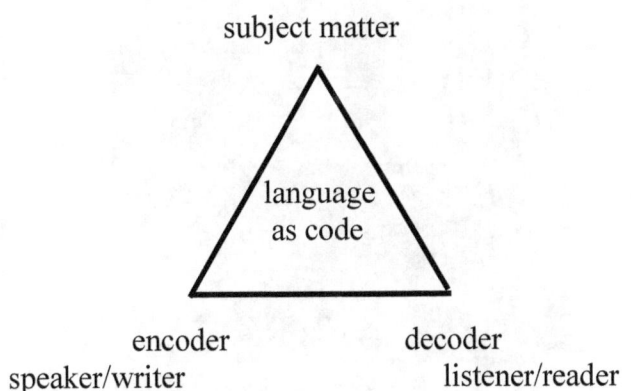

[16] If this becomes too much of a problem for you, try using another coding system; try putting your ideas into dance or sculpture or harp sounds to transfer them to others.

Delivery.

Ahhh. At the conclusion of the successful road-trip you find yourself all safe and sound, coming down just "where you want to be" (Quakers) – and likewise for the successful writing experience. In concluding, you can recall where you've been and how those concepts add up to where you are. Even better, you can note how the place to which you've come is its own place—made possible by the journey to all the other places along the way—but, still, its own place. That is, your conclusion can grow from "in light of this and that and the other thing, I told you so about the thesis"[17] to "we know how we got here and here we are." As you conclude your journey, you really should revisit your relationship with your companions—turn touchy moments to good feelings. Rather than just repeating how you started out, or tracing where you've visited, you can draw a conclusion from where you've traveled. So, you are in control of your writing experience. Make it a good one.

© Everett Historical/Shutterstock.com

---

[17] Which does work sometimes.

Cicero begins *De Inventione* with a piece too nice to gloss over:

> I. I have often turned over and over in my mind this question—whether fluency in language and eloquence have been more beneficial or more harmful to citizens and cultures. For when I consider the disasters of our republic, and when I consider the calamities of ancient important states, I see that a significant part of their hardship and distress has begun with the conduct and words of their most eloquent men. At the same time, when I look back on documents and written memorials that extend older than any personal memory, I see that many cities have been established, that many wars have been resolved, and that many enduring alliances and friendships have been cemented by deliberate wisdom that was assisted by eloquence. Pondering for some time the interplay of language and history, I conclude that wisdom without eloquence is of little advantage to states. Furthermore, eloquence without wisdom can cause great harm both to states and to the populace.
>
> Those who neglect the most virtuous and honorable considerations of wisdom and duty, and instead devote themselves merely to the study and practice of speaking, train themselves to become useless and potentially harmful to their country. On the other hand, those who study eloquence, so as to benefit their country and advocate for the public good will be citizens of the greatest service to themselves and to general social interests through devotion to their country.
>
> The origin of this thing called eloquence—whether it be a study, or an art, or some particular training, or some natural faculty—arises from most honorable causes, and proceeds on the most excellent principles.
>
> IV. Nonetheless, citizens ought to devote themselves to the study of eloquence even though, historically, some have misused it in both private and

public affairs. All should study eloquence in order to prevent the wicked from injuring the good and causing calamity to the country. Only the study of language can protect citizens in private and public to maintain a life that is safe, honorable, noteworthy, and pleasant. For from eloquence, the state receives the greatest advantages and only if based in wisdom, that governor of all human affairs.[18]

Nice way to begin. Cicero then briefly describes each of the parts (or steps) that we can use to create good discourse: *inventio*, *dispositio*, *elocutio*, *memoria*, and *pronuntiatio*:

Invention[19] is finding or developing true or probable topics which may make one's cause appear probable. Arrangement[20] is the distribution of topics (thus discovered) into a regular and logical order. Elocution[21] is putting the invented and ordered ideas into suitable words and sentences. Memory[22] is the lasting sense in the mind of these ideas and words. Delivery[23] is regulating the voice and body in a way that reflects the dignity of the subject matter and the style.[24]

---

[18] Interpreted from *The Treatise by M.T. Cicero on Rhetorical Invention* (or *De Inventione*). Translated by C.D. Yonge. George Bell & Sons, York Street, Covent Garden, London. 1890.
[19] Again, note that "invention" more properly means "discovery" by exploring your subject.
[20] Given the Latin "*dispositio*," arrangement might more properly mean "positioning."
[21] Most current writing texts call this "style."
[22] This sense of memory extends beyond mindless memorization as we know it.
[23] This chapter will explore and approach delivery not in terms of oral discourse, but in terms of writing.
[24] Interpreted from *The Treatise by M.T. Cicero on Rhetorical Invention* (or *De Inventione*). Translated by C.D. Yonge. George Bell & Sons, York Street, Coventry Garden, London. 1890.

And so we proceed. You gather material; you arrange it; you embed the arranged material into words; you revise and edit to ensure your mental grasp of the matter and words; you put the work into a form that will be well received well in your particular discourse community. By following Cicero's method you can efficiently and effectively produce a piece of writing. The next chapters show how.

III

Invention

or

How to Gather Your Materials

Before you can write an essay or paper, you need first gather materials and information. Cicero begins his discussion of how to gather materials by showing that every speech, essay, debate, etc. contains some sort of issue. We can gather information about particular issues by trying to pin-point certain "questions." Issues commonly involve questions of **fact** or **definition**, or the **nature of an act**, or the **legal processes**. By exploring the situation of the issue through these questions, we can often figure out what to think and say. And in the process, we often come up with a lot of material to use.

You can gather information for writing about issues involving questions of fact or definition by following Plato's old method of repeatedly asking "huh?" in conversation with someone or with yourself. The Latin sense of the word "definition" has a high school football sense to it as through struggle we can try to run around (or find out about) the apparent end of something. By doing end-runs around conceptual blockers we can gain yardage. Whatever we find out about may be useful in explaining and persuading. So look beyond the apparent blocked ends of words and concepts as they fly by you.

"Hey, Jen; I got a summer job with the Forest Service."
"Huh?"
"You know the forest, Man—like woods, like where the wild things are."
"Yeah, but what's the 'Service' bit? Like who's getting served—humans or critters?"

Or—

"Hey, Jen; got a new major: Wildlife Management."

"Huh?"

"Come on, Man, deal with it; go look it up; it is what it is; get with it; gimme a break."

"Naah, I don't get it. How can you *manage* something called '*wild*' life?"

"Huh?"

"Like who needs managing—critters or humans?"

Or—

"Say, Jen; I gave it all up, like you say about managing. I'm going into administration."

"Cool. Get me an iced mocha, double, not too heavy on the whipped cream."

"Say what!?"

"You said, 'administration'?"

"Huh?"

"Latin, Bozo; '*ministrare*'—to serve. So start serving."

We get to questions that focus on the nature of an act when we finally agree on the definition of the issue and agree on what an act has involved or will involve.[1] We then begin to explore questions about how important the issue/act is or about the issue's or act's quality. Is it just or unjust; profitable or unprofitable? This is called a dialectic process of questioning and you can turn the page to see how to do this thing.

"So, Jen; to deal with you, I'm taking this course in rhetoric."

"Yeah, well, what good is it?"

---

[1] In case anyone is trying to follow Cicero in the original, we're up to Book I, Chapter VIII, section IX.

Furthermore, we can explore the nature of the issue or act in terms of its intrinsic value or in terms of how it fits into customs or utility or the legal system. We can ask whether something is valuable in and of itself or whether its value comes vis-à-vis "the system."

> "Well, this new rhetoric course fits into my new triple major of forestry, wildlife management, and public administration."
>
> "Doyle, have you ever considered learning something?"

The Essay Assignment
Picking a Topic Vs. Developing a Topic

Perhaps you might be getting some urge to try out some of these classical ideas for creating better arguments relative to some issue that has perhaps been bothering you. For example, if your room-mate annoys you by leaving unwashed dishes in the sink, you might try to figure out what in that habit causes the annoyance. So you use dialectics—

> Damn, look at this kitchen—a veritable health hazard.
>
> [So what are the elements/implications of this circumstance?]
>
> I suppose that she expects me to wash all these dishes.
>
> [So what are the elements/implications of this circumstance?]
>
> Expecting me to put her stuff away and wash her dishes isn't cool.
>
> [So what are the elements/implications of this circumstance?]
>
> People should clean up their own messes.
>
> [So what are the elements/implications of this circumstance?]
>
> People should feel responsible for their own actions.
>
> Hey, that's it. I'll write about social responsibility!

By using this procedure, you aren't really "picking a topic" out of the air; rather, you're "developing" something to write about. You might feel closer to whatever you come up with through this process, because you directed the development your subject. Rather than trying to create some alien pseudo-academic voice, using dialectics will give YOU a "voice" in your essay.

Historically, writing theorists and teachers have noticed that students who develop issues of their own concern as subjects for their essays learn to write a bit more easily and learn to write better as well.[2] Generally, students have greater interest in and actually care about subjects that they develop themselves. In caring about their subjects, students might feel more inclined to care more about expressing and communicating. And so they might put more energy into the writing process.

So give it a try. In order to practice the many ideas for writing presented here, begin to develop a concern of your own. Think of the last time you felt agitated or felt strongly about something. Think of something that concerns you right now. Think about what you love (or hate) to do. Then use Plato's method of focusing on some pivotal term or terms relative to your issue. Begin breaking your concern or issue down into its various features and/or elements. To help you work with this method, on the next page are some blanks in which you can explore the elements and implications of your own concern.

---

[2] For a greater explanation regarding the importance of students developing their own concerns as subjects for practice essays, see such rhetoricians on the subject as
- Richard Whately, D.D., *Elements of Rhetoric* [*Comprising the Substance of the Article in the Encyclopædia Metropolitana with Additions, &c.*], Boston: James Munroe and Co., 1839, (17-22).
- Gertrude Buck, Ph.D., "Recent Tendencies in the Teaching of English Composition" as reprinted in *Toward a Feminist Rhetoric: The Writing of Gertrude Buck*, ed. Joann Campbell, University of Pittsburgh Press, 1996, (91-95). Buck provides various answers for the question, "How can natural conditions of writing be substituted in the schoolroom for artificial?"

Plato and others since him offer this strategy for discovering greater and greater "truths" about things. In Plato's view, we should always know everything we can know about a subject before trying to talk about it.[3]

© alex74/Shutterstock.com

---

[3] This concept has grave consequences for modern T.V. and radio talk shows.

How to Use Dialectics to Figure Things Out

⟵ Put your own pivotal concept here

Name two elements of your concept here

See if you can come up with other ways of naming the elements of your pivotal concept.

Now begin to focus on just one feature of your term ⟶

Then proceed to break this one aspect down into *its* various parts.

Put your favorite One here.

Then break that down.

Then explore those aspects. And draw your own arrows to their various factors.

And then show further elements and implications for each of the preceding factors.

A.
B.

A.
B.

A.
B.

And so on! Do continue —

Interlude Regarding the History of Invention

Through history, invention has certainly had its share of voices feeding into how to think about it. Remember that the 400-300 BCE Greeks had pictured truth as an existent, but often hidden, gift of the gods. To *find* elusive truths, an earthly person used some "heuristic" or other—like dialectic (breaking the issue down into parts trying to examine each part)—to get to it. The Greeks had great respect for the truth so trying to *create* truth was a bad, if not unthinkable, thing to do. When the Romans got hold of heuristic, however, they changed it to "inventio" or "invention"; truth, as the gift of the gods, lost some of its mystique and sacredness and the method of coming into truth became more utilitarian. Whereas the Greek Aristotle had envisioned gathering materials as "topoi" or "places to go" or ways of seeking various perspectives, the Romans spoke of invention as gathering up a "copia" of materials for writing some speech or essay—with a hint of aggression as (you may recall) the Latin "copia" means all the supplies in the wagon that help soldiers make war—like ammo, extra shoelaces, blankets, food, pots & pans, etc.[4] By the time of St. Augustine, heuristics-turned-invention takes on one another sense. Figuring out what to say about something becomes dependent on the grace of God for divine inspiration.[5] One could, however, study the scriptures and try to figure for oneself what all the signs in the various stories and parables mean.[6] On the other side of the middle ages, invention goes out the window altogether and lands in the lap of "science." But that's another story.

---

[4] Ammo and shoelaces? Question authority.
[5] Many students commonly use this technique of invention, waiting for some divine inspiration to hit and enable them to write an essay at three a.m. the night before it's due. This technique does not work without the spiritual commitment advocated by St. Augustine.
[6] This figuring out of scripture signs is called an even bigger "h" word—hermeneutics.

While sometimes invention resulted from playing with logic, concepts of reasoning and logic itself danced around a bit. Invention and logic in the time of the Greeks had the sense that knowledge and truth were derived from/led out from/deduced from what was already known. To draw particular knowledge from what is already generally known is called "deduction." For example, by deductive reasoning I could draw on experience and common knowledge to figure that if it's cold and rainy down here at the base of a mountain, it must be snowing up on top.

On the other side of the middle ages thinking gradually began to reject the intuitive, prior knowledge-based deduction in favor of induction—scientific experiment.[7] People could figure out their own truths and knowledge by poking around with their senses. Looking at things through weird shaped glass revealed many new "facts" that contradicted what everyone had always known—like there were bugs in dirt and maybe the sun rather than the earth was the center of the cosmos. Such a major change in the way a whole culture bases its assumptions is called a "paradigm shift."

> So, what's a "paradigm"?
> A way of thinking that everyone just commonly accepts is called a "paradigm." Thinking inductively sure did "subvert the dominant paradigm."[8] People accustomed to drawing their answers from commonly held beliefs began to wonder what knowledge was all about. And some people got themselves into big trouble with institutions—like the church—that didn't want people to switch ways of thinking (paradigms).

---

[7] For example, by making a bunch of calls and doing meteorological experiments I could find out if it's snowing up on top of the mountain.

[8] As says the bumper sticker encouraging us to confront the accepted dominant assumptions of our culture.

Interestingly, we have happened into history at a time when both deductive and inductive thought have at least been thought of. And so you can use either sort of reasoning or even both sorts to determine the basis of your argument—or to think for that matter.

SOME CURRENT CONVENTIONAL INVENTION STRATEGIES
(THAT YOU'VE PROBABLY ALREADY HEARD ABOUT)

Current writing texts usually provide several schemes by which students can gather information. Here's a quick run-down of compositionists' additions to what you've already learned using dialectics.

The Journalist's W's.

Like the Five or Six Nations of the Iroquois and seven or eight defendants in the Chicago Eight (?) Trial, the numbers of W's seem elusive. The idea here follows the old idea of questioning to find (develop?) more information, but this particular system gives you specific places to go or cues for asking your questions. Journalists (supposedly) commonly use these cues for gathering information for writing news stories. Simple: just ask relative to your issue or situation a bunch of "w" questions—who, what, when, where, why, how?[9] That is, given any situation, you can ask, who is involved? What is the nature of the act or issue? When did/does/will this act/issue

---

[9] Hey, it ends with a "w."

happen? Where did/does/will this act/issue happen? Why did/does/will[10] this act/issue happen? And how? Exploring these aspects of something will reveal a bunch of information that you can further explore and eventually use in your essay.

Kenneth Burke's Pentad.

Drawing on the premise that all the world's a stage,[11] Burke reflects Cicero's concern with exploring the intrinsic nature of things. He shows that by questioning the motives of situations, we can learn more about them. We ponder motives by asking the nature of a "pentad": Act, Scene, Agent, Agency and Purpose. And so we can learn more about a situation and/or something's circumstances, by

- Naming the Act—naming "what took place in thought or deed";
- Naming the Scene—naming "the background of the act, the situation in which it occurred";
- Indicating the Agent—indicating "what person or kind of person (agent) performed the act";
- Indicating the Agency—indicating "what means or instruments" the agent used;
- Exploring the Purpose—examining the various philosophic and human motivations for the act or situation.[12]

---

[10] Some languages do not have these pesky verb tenses. While verb tenses may give us information regarding time, they also seem to dam up life's gift, the natural resource, time. In dialects that do not put time into tense-cages we can say, "Yesterday, I go to the beach. Today I go to the beach. Tomorrow I go to the beach." Perhaps verb tenses do strange things to our conceptualization of being. Contemplate language.

[11] So say Shakespeare (*As You Like It*, Act II, Scene 7) and Elvis ("Are You Lonesome Tonight?").

[12] For more, see Burke's *A Grammar of Motives*.

Both the journalist's "w's" and Burke's dramatism or pentad give us specific cues for exploring an issue. Note the similarities:

who? ⟷ Agent

what? ⟷ Act

when? ⟵
where? ⟷ Scene

why? ⟷ Purpose

how? ⟷ Agency

In regards to Cicero's observation that we can experience things variously—sometimes catching the more utilitarian or legal vibes or sometimes catching the more philosophic or humanist vibes—maybe we should use all of these aspects of inquiry. Then we can go further and, taking a cue from Burke, ask questions based on the natural interdependency of these various areas of investigation.

Clustering/Mapping.

Gabrielle Rico has written a textbook[13] and popularized a way of gathering information by forcing ourselves to ask "huh?" as cued by associated ideas. We put an idea in a circle and then try to come up with a bunch more ideas related to the one in the circle. Then we try to come up with ideas related to each of the originally

---

[13] *Writing on the Right Side of the Brain.*

related ideas. And so on and so on, gathering lots of aspects of things in a sort of dialectic.

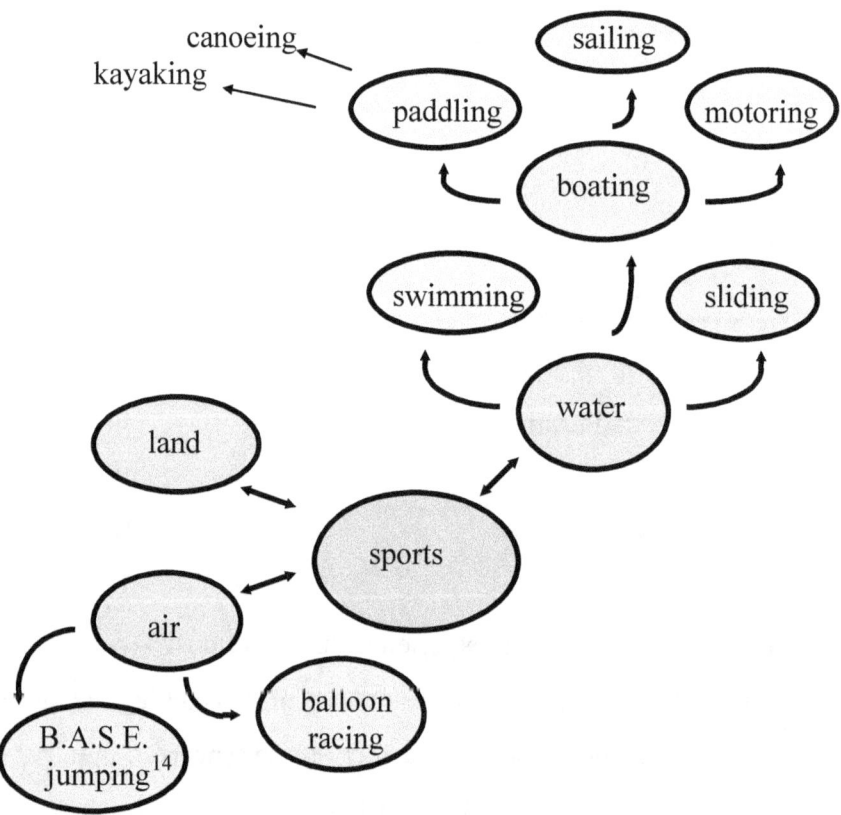

As with Burke, these associated ideas should flow from our human or philosophical or psychological motivation rather than from empirical experiment. In other words, this scheme of inquiry works by deduction—literally leading[15] away from the general toward the specific.

---

[14] B.A.S.E. stands for "Bridge, Antennae, Span, Earth." With respect to Dean Potter and Graham Hunt, who died in final flying from Taft Point, Yosemite National Park, California, May 16, 2015.
[15] Remember "ducio" to lead, roughly related to heating ducts?

You have probably already experienced this sense of mapping or clustering as you have surfed the internet.[16] Clicking on an icon or word sends you to various new sites for information. Presumably each click onto an icon brings you closer to what you are looking for. By surfing the net aimlessly for hours, however, you have probably also learned that "sometimes you get the bear and sometimes the bear gets you."[17] That is, despite your activity to find some materials, sometimes attempts prove futile.

Outlining.

Now over on the other side of the brain,[18] we can begin with the order and have the order itself drive our inquiry. Remember the outline?

    I. Big thing.

        A. Less big thing.

            1. Even smaller thing.

            2. Another smaller thing.

        B. Another less big thing.

---

[16] Thanks to student Shiow-Chen Lin for pointing out to me the similarities between clustering and surfing the internet.
[17] Memorable saying from Joel Stratte, Stanford University, 1968, who predated its use in the movie, *The Big Lebowski* (1998).
[18] Perhaps. Some studies now challenge the right & left brain business.

Well, look what you can do with your clustering.

    I. Sports.

        A. Water sports.

            1. Swimming.

            2. Sliding.

            3. Boating.

                a. Motoring.

                b. Sailing.

                c. Paddling.

                    i. Canoeing.

                    ii. Kayaking.

        B. Land sports.

        C. Air sports.

            1. Balloon racing.

            2. B.A.S.E. jumping.

And so on. Notice that the clustering scheme of drawing bubbles to put your ideas into can easily—poof—turn into an outline. Very importantly, realize that this sort of outline fun may be great for helping you discover new information, but has absolutely nothing—zip, nada—to do with organizing your paper. First, you gather your materials. Then you organize those materials according to criteria (like your clueless and demanding readers) that have little to do with outlines because outlines are not human.[19] [Just wait until you get to Chapter IV, regarding arrangement.]

---

[19] It may do you some good to outline an already written piece of writing, but it does little good to outline your brain and then create a piece of writing accordingly.

Tagmemics.

Writing theorists have borrowed systems of inquiry from various domains from philosophy to physics. One system borrowed from physics, called tagmemics, provides us with still another way of looking at situations. This system encourages us to look at some thing or issue as if it were a particle, a wave, and a field. You might find this embarrassedly simplified version helpful. Hang on.

Particle. Thinking of your issue as a particle within a larger system, you can investigate how it fits into that larger system. This view includes the old high school "compare and contrast" paper, but you can extend this view to include the *ways* a phenomenon functions within a field. Like, how do roses fit into your garden or how do the writings of Malcolm X fit into American literature or how does American literature fit into American culture. How does Dixieland Jazz fit in to the history and philosophy of American music—

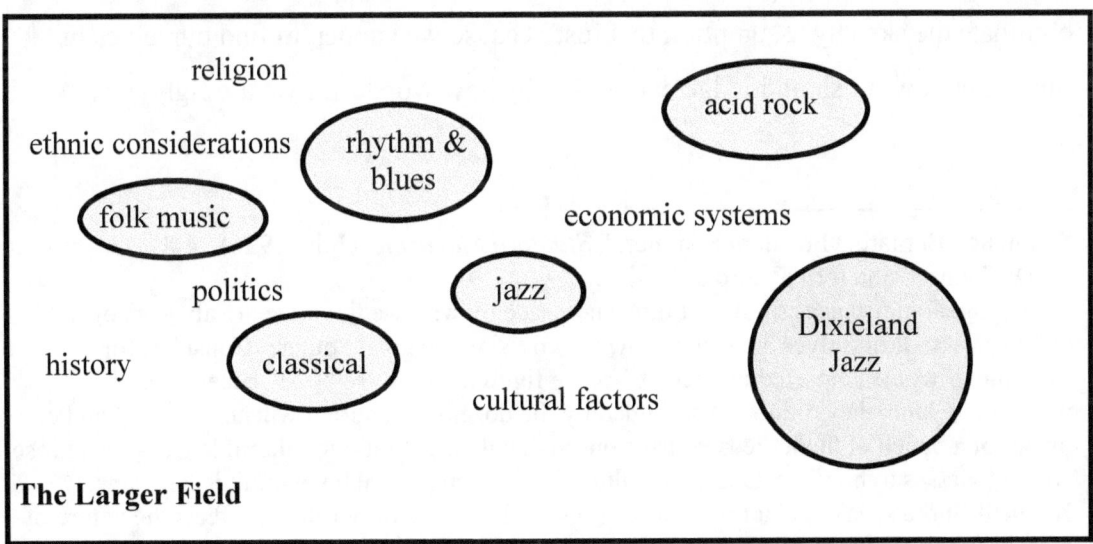

Wave. Thinking of your issue as a wave, you can investigate how your issue changes through time and circumstances. Like those (then) crazy kids who went south to register voters in the early 1960s were later exonerated and celebrated as heroes in such publications as *The Stanford Magazine*.[20] You can explore the factors feeding into that change of public opinion and how changing public opinion has spawned subsequent developments. Or you might investigate how popular music has developed and changed amid other changing influences.

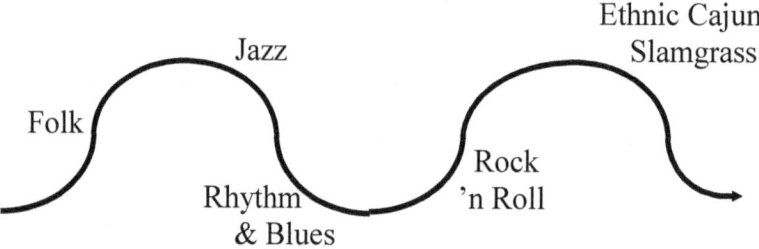

Looking at some circumstance as it changes through time is called a "diachronic"[21] view. Accepting that everything keeps on changing for better and/or for worse helps eliminate the sketchy assumption that just because we happen to find ourselves in time right now we should judge everything by how wonderful we are right now.[22]

---

[20] Butcher, Bernard. "Freedom Summer." *Stanford Magazine.* (July, 1996) 74-81.
[21] "Dia" – back and forth; "chrono" – time.
[22] Judging circumstances of distant time and space by who we think we are always depends on our vision of ourselves as well as how we envision the great "other." Consider, for example, if women closeted in ancient Greece figured they were "free" because unlike women in China, they didn't get strangled by the dozens and buried whenever a husband or owner of a bunch of them died. Perhaps our vision depends on our cultural lenses—from rose colored glasses to blinders. One such cultural lens through which we think is language. Kenneth Burke speaks of "terministic screens": "the nature of our terms affects the nature of our observations, in the sense that the terms direct the attention to one field rather than to another." From *Language as Symbolic Action*, (46). Watch, then, how people use language to name things before even getting to know what they are talking about.

Field. Thinking of your issue as a field, you can explore the various elements that make it what it is. Like you can explore the various elements of geriatric nursing or running a white water rafting operation. You can explore the various elements of American music:

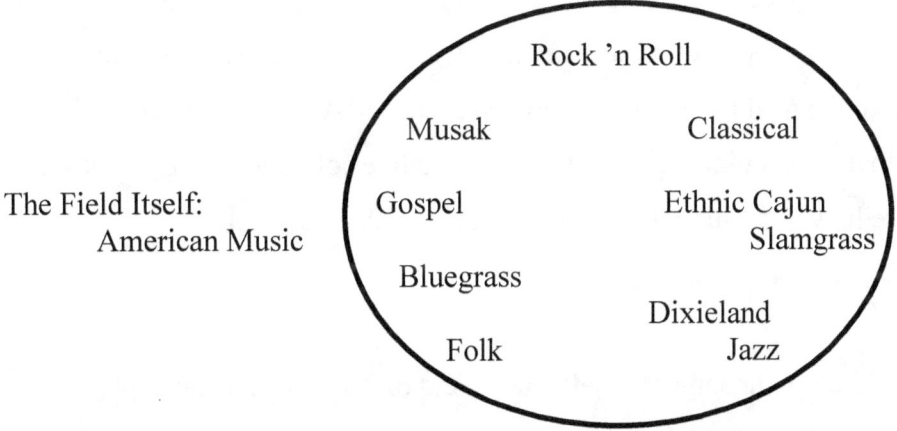

You can consider an entire field not only as it exists right now, but also at any one point in time. For example you can consider the various players and elements of Jazz on one morning in Harlem, New York.[23]

PIZZA THEORY.

If this simplified version of tagmemics seems a cumbersome way of exploring your subject, you might think of the system as pizzas.

Particle. If you consider your subject first as exemplary of other such subjects, you can compare that whole subject to other whole subjects —just as you might compare

---

[23] As did the recent documentary, *A Great Day in Harlem*.

a Domino's pizza to one from Pizza Hut or from that nice Italian restaurant and from next door neighbor, Tony's mom, Mrs. Scardina's fresh fish pizza.

Wave. If you consider your subject, then, in terms of its development and history, you can treat your subject as an aging pizza—it was really huge and hot and juicy two nights ago before Mario spilled his beer on the anchovy side; then when I took it out of the refrigerator the next morning it resembled a Frisbee stuck to cardboard; at lunch the part that the cat didn't get tasted OK if you like cold oiled dough. Just so, you can observe how any situation or phenomenon develops through a big view of history or through a shorter view.

Field. If you consider your subject, finally, as a field of its own, you can explore it as you might explore what appears to make up a particular pizza. There's some alleged cheese and mystery meat and red stuff. You can explore further to determine just what "cheese food" and that strange "meat" is. Just so, you can explore beyond the appearances of what factors comprise your subject to delve deeper and deeper into just what is going on.

Freewriting. (So called.)

Rumor has it that judges often don't know what to make of some cases until they begin to write about them. Forcing ourselves to write about something often forces us to start thinking about the thing we have to write about. As you begin to write randomly about your subject, you ask yourself questions and then attempt answers. To encourage thinking, some teachers even assign journal writing.

Hints for freewriting and writing in journals:

- Omit references to your own brilliance. Try to explore your own thoughts without focusing on just you. That is, focus on whatever you're supposed to be focusing on.
- Move beyond summary. A person can quite easily summarize something without thinking about it. With earphones pumping the mind full of complex rhythms and lyrics, a person can use eyeballs to remove ideas from a page, send them bypassing the brain to the fingers, and squirt them right out the end of the pen. Do not do this. Your mission here is to **think** about your issue and then explore what you think by commingling your thoughts with language.[24]
- Now that you're thinking, move beyond simple judgment—"Hawthorne is a good writer." Rather, consider issues about your subject—"Hawthorne keeps having crazy scientists kill off beautiful young women characters; how come?"

INTERLUDE FOR EXPLANATION:
COLLEGE

Yes, these hints may certainly involve a major revelation, identity crisis, and paradigm shift. By now you've probably figured out that there is some very real, but unspoken difference between college and high school (or the business world for that matter). Oddly, this unspoken difference that you sense has to do with historical and conceptual differences in how people consider the size of books.

---

[24] This is called the epistemic process.

When you were in high school (or out in the business world), books were big and you were little. You took notes from the books because they were written and, so, correct.[25] If you took homemaking classes in the 1960s, you took notes on the importance of the four food groups[26] (all dependent on agri-business) and how to make men feel good about themselves. If you took history class from Coach Dodson, you took notes on the dates and places of every W.W. II battle and that was history.

Going to college you face a whole new game plan. Yes, like high school, in college you still need to know all the stuff in the books. But in college you need to do more than just learn the stuff in books—you need to think about it too. Now this gets scary because thinking about what you learn can cause you to change—your identity and your behavior. And it gets scarier because you don't know who you will change into before you read and learn something so you can't knowledgeably decide what or what not or whether or whether not to read and think. This is why teachers often assign readings. They have read stuff and thought about it and changed and have discovered that the thinking-induced change is good nourishment or medicine. So you have to trust or respect that experience. More scary still: as you read and think, you may have to let go of some of the ideas that are a comfortable part of you. That is, learning and thinking can bring pain as well as insight and enlightenment.[27]

To make matters worse, while the books and the thoughts inside them have grown even bigger with the power to change you, some of your teachers tell you that

---

[25] A concept brought to us by 1700's rhetorician, Richard Whately. Revisited more recently by poet, Kenneth Patchen in *Because It Is*, page 38:
> [The little green blackbird] had some cards printed and
> Handed them out. This of course started
> A war, because the cards were printed
> With ink.

[26] Meats, grains, dairy products, vegetables & fruits. Different from the four food groups observed by *San Francisco Chronicle* columnist Herb Caen: sugar, alcohol, caffeine, and grease.

[27] Plato speaks of this pain and sight and light in his parable of the cave in *The Republic*.

you must be bigger than those thoughts that are messing with your mind. Teachers say things like, "read the chapter and get a handle on it." You suddenly find yourself in the impossibly contradictory situation of, on the one hand, having to think and change and, on the other hand, of having to make some definitive statement that shows you are now bigger than all those books that are playing tug of war in your head. Furthermore, the academic situation expects you to use those very books to support/illustrate your now big and controlling brilliant idea.[28]

Something like this shift in the power and function of books also happened to the whole of culture sometime between the 1850s and now. In the old days books were bigger than people and "gripped" them and "good" books **changed** their readers. The whole idea of reading was to learn and grow and help a reader develop into a somewhat ideal identity. That is, books could help people develop themselves toward a community held sense of self—a community and/or national ethos.[29] In the past century the idea of being an individual has gone from being impolite (as setting one's self apart from and perhaps even above contributing to the community) to the idea of being an individual as acceptable. Since we now consider self-esteem as a good thing (rather than as a lack of humility), we often just want to observe the ideas in books and stay who we are as we read them: "Hey, I like myself just fine like I am. Just let me read this stuff and tell me what I'm supposed to do for an 'A'." Since a larger proportion of teachers think the old way (that books are bigger than readers) and a larger proportion of students think this new way (that readers are bigger than books), teachers and students often think past each other.[30]

---

[28] Your author does not know what to make of all this, but does sympathize with your academia-induced feelings of anguish. It's OK, you're OK; you're just in an odd situation, but it's a good odd situation, so you might as well enjoy it.
[29] See, you can use words like that now.
[30] As Bob Dylan put it, "I was so much older then; I'm younger than that now."

Using freewriting, you need to consider your stance as a student. Yes, you can learn and grow from new information, but at the same time you should think about the information you are gathering. Furthermore, remember—(like the comment on outlining above) this freewriting is **not** your essay. Given the old message/writer/reader triangle, writing without considering your reader is somewhat egotistical or writer-centered. Whatever material you produced through the freewriting process you will eventually use to create a reader-centered (reader readable!) piece. How to do that comes in Cicero's next steps—especially arrangement and style. But first, just one more invention strategy—expanding what you know as well as what you can use to communicate.

A VERY OLD & TRADITIONAL AMERICAN INVENTION STRATEGY: THE MEDICINE WHEEL

Since each of us has a unique past and body,[31] we tend to observe and conceptualize phenomena in unique ways. The idea of the Medicine Wheel[32] extends the idea that

---

[31] Possible/shaky exception: identical twins share the same genetic determinants. Sometimes identical twins—even apart from one another—perceive phenomena similarly.

[32] Your author's apology. Native American writer and speaker, Sherman Alexie, urges us not to appropriate the spirituality of other peoples, but to deal with our own traditional spirituality. Accordingly, the author here does not present the traditional Native American Medicine Wheel in its proper spiritual context because the author's tradition and experience lies outside that spirituality. Coming from a "Scande-whovian" heritage of utility and practicality, the author attaches a sense of utility and practicality to a cultural tradition meant to engender wonder and wisdom and inter-personal/inter-environmental respect. That is, your author purposefully avoids the current Euro-American "wannabe" trend to usurp Native spirituality into a commodity for the spiritually starved. I avoid mentioning the spiritual sense of the Medicine Wheel to avoid diminishing that sense or just getting it wrong or putting into print what should properly remain in memory (see Chapter VI, "Memory or Keeping Your Head Together"). What you have here is not spirituality, but a psychological system that

each of us sees everything differently from one another. Using this ancient source of wisdom, we can understand and respect why not everyone perceives as we do. Using The Medicine Wheel as an invention strategy, we can also struggle[33] to perceive in ways additional to how we customarily perceive. As you'll see in the next chapter (about arrangement), perceiving phenomena in multiple ways enables a writer to communicate more effectively with readers who perceive differently from the writer and from one another.

Essentially, we perceive in an infinite circle of methods. Although this circle focuses on four primary directions and/or cognitive methods, as the primary colors mix to produce the spectrum, so the four primary cognitive methods mix to produce the spectrum of human sensibility. This said, add the factor of time—variations of history, of day, of age, of the moment. Amid the infinite variations of the spectrum we do name colors, and amid the variations of human sensibility we name certain types.[34]

Interestingly, many ancient peoples—including the Greeks and the Native Americans—spoke of cognition and perception in terms of direction. The Greeks spoke of topoi—"places to go" to pursue ways to think of something. The Medicine Wheel comes to us in terms of four directions: North, South, East, and West. Also, as other ancient wisdom comes to us through parables of animals or what we might currently call "magical realism," the Medicine Wheel comes to us in signs or symbols

---

often attends spiritual wisdom—much as George Campbell's psychologically oriented philosophy of rhetoric attends his primary work as a Christian theologian (see Chapter VI of the sequel to this book, *Classical Rhetoric Now!*).

[33] In "The Parable of the Cave" in *The Republic*, Plato portrays people as slaves chained down by outside forces (cultural? economic?) to perceive only shadows of what is really going on. Breaking the chains that restrict our perception requires a tremendous struggle. Looking beyond the shadows and into the light of truth can be painful.

[34] In this respect, naming colors and naming human characteristics are both pretty inaccurate and do damage to their respective spectrums.

that communicate to visually-oriented as well as to language-oriented learners. The stories and wisdom of the Medicine Wheel, therefore, appeal to people of various ages and means of perception.[35]

As put by Hyemeyohsts Storm,

In many ways this Circle, the Medicine Wheel, can best be understood if you think of it as a mirror in which everything is reflected. "The Universe is the Mirror of the People," the old Teachers tell us, "and each person is a Mirror to every other person."

Any idea, person or object can be a Medicine Wheel, a Mirror, for us. The tiniest flower can be such a Mirror, as can a wolf, a story, a touch, a religion or a mountain top. For example, one person alone on a mountain top at night might feel fear. Another might feel calm and peaceful. Still another might feel lonely, and a fourth person might feel nothing at all. In each case the mountain top would be the same, but it would be perceived differently as it reflected the feelings of the different people who experienced it. (*Seven Arrows*, pages 4-5)

---

[35] Wouldn't it be nice if all our current wisdom-bearing texts so appealed to such a wide audience—beyond the linguistic confines established by those privileged to have learned to code and decode the rarefied codes of academia.

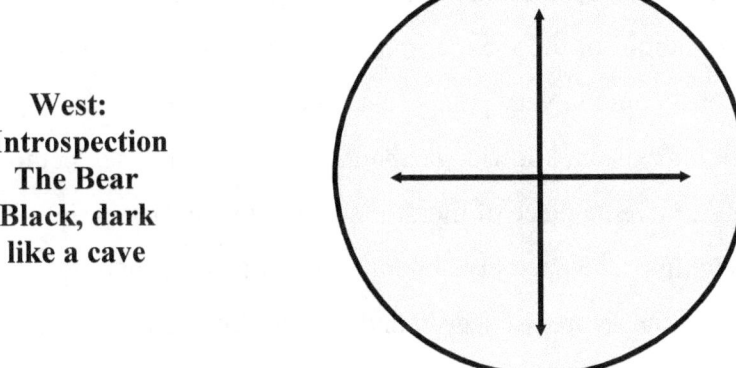

North: Wisdom
The Buffalo   Silvery, white, cold

West:
Introspection
The Bear
Black, dark
like a cave

East:
Illumination
The Eagle
Golden, bright
like the Sunrise

South: Trust and Innocence
The Mouse   Green

The Mouse.

↝ The mouse person sees things close up. Often innocently trusting the first touch of the whiskers, the mouse person quickly gets right into close details.

The Bear.

↝ The bear person perceives things introspectively with a real heartfelt connection to things. Encountering something, the bear ponders it reflectively, drawing on memory, intuition, and imagination.

The Buffalo.

↝ The buffalo person relies on cold wisdom to perceive things. Encountering an idea, the buffalo feels the need to know all about it, but often lacks introspective or tangible connection to the object of perception.

The Eagle.

↝ The eagle person perceives things in terms of a broad sweeping overview. The eagle easily makes generalizations and abstractions, but often can't see the details that might propel the generalizations.

The Mouse. ☞ Some people, then, jump to conclusions quickly, persuading themselves and others of things by heaping details upon details. Here we have the image of wild-eyed engineers or scientists so involved with experiments to have not considered the general ramifications of those experiments—they "can't see the forest for the trees." Moving nervously among very precise data and ideas, the mouse people often neglect to look for existent knowledge about things and often neglect to slow down and ponder things. Given a piece of literature, these students jump right in and start measuring and weighing. They perceive literature in terms of its internal evidence[36] and can pick out all the figures of speech and meters. Although they can point out all the constituent parts of a piece of literature, they often have difficulty getting close to it. They have a very difficult time coming up with some thesis or general statement about literature and since they have spent so much time figuring out what makes a piece "tick,"[37] they rarely feel inclined to consult critics or sources who might put the piece within some larger (like historical or economic) context.

The Bear. ☞ Other people rely quite comfortably on their own reflections. They approach ideas and phenomena ready to relate just about any circumstances to their own lives. Often these people can't explain why they feel so strongly about things; they sense when things are right or wrong, but can't communicate why in terms of actual data or how others might have investigated similar situations. Given that same piece of literature, introspective bear persons characteristically feel an author speaking to them.[38] They react with tears or laughter or pity and feel that other modes of perception fall short of feeling the real passion of a piece.

---

[36] We might call these people "New Critical" readers.
[37] As if it's a piece of machinery.
[38] We might call these people "reader-response" readers.

The Buffalo. 🐃 Still other people lack this trust in their own reflections of things and turn, instead, to "experts." These people seek to learn all *about* a situation, but don't get to the heart of the matter as do the mouse sorts. Given that same piece of literature, these students make a beeline to the library and struggle to put the piece into a larger context of its historical/cultural/economic/etc. significance.[39] These students can actually learn all about a piece of literature without even reading the thing and, for some strange reason, our system usually rewards them more than the bear students who read
so ponderously.

The Eagle. 🦅 Finally, some people feel very comfortable making big brash, and often unsubstantiated, statements. Drawing on personal strength rather than evidence, these people often back their assertions with the word, "obviously." These students have no trouble at all making thesis statements, but then write very short papers complaining that they can't find any material or that they don't need any material to illustrate or explain their perceptions. Given that same piece of literature, these students immediately blurt out judgments or one-liners meant to cubby-hole or qualify the piece according to their judgments. These students sometimes even mean their qualifying statements to diminish the piece of literature and place themselves above it. Naturally, among other non-eagle people, this usually backfires.

---

[39] We might call these people Marxist critics.

So four students take a break from school to go see a movie, and find they have very different reactions to what appears to be the same experience.

⚔ Rhett: Whoa, did you catch the work in this film? Such precision. Those buttons on the general's vest musta been real, with their little scrolling of ivy on the edges. And the amazing music: you could just catch the lyrics and put 'em together with what the general was saying at the same time, and the meter of the lyrics worked too perfectly with that cat under the table—the twitch-beat of its tail and the . . . .

🐟 Jan: Whaaaaaaaaaah— What are you goin on about? Didn't it (snuffle) just kill you when . . . whaaaaaaaah. I mean, when she realized deep down that (snuffle, blow) . . . . ohhhhh . . . how could that insensitive idiot even consider whaaaaaaaahhhh . . . ✈ Pat: Now really. If you'd all just settle down, you'd recall that when this film came out in the fall of 1990, the available technology was limited in terms of . . . .

⚡ Wade: Dumb film man, real dumb. Anyone hungry? I know a place open down on Third that does a dynomite . . . .

🐟 Jan: How can you even think of eating when that poor starving little boy . . . . snuffle, whaaaaaaaaah.

⚔ Rhett: Whaddaya mean, dumb? Like how? Where? The thing was totally perfect in every detail. Did you see the embroidery in that curtain behind that chair with the hand-carving under the arms? That embroidery matched perfectly with the stained glass at the other guy's house in the next to last scene.

✈ Pat: Certainly the judges at Cannes didn't think it was dumb the next year when they compared it with that third work by Desi's son-in-law—you know, the one that was filmed half in Kenya and half in L.A. on a budget three times what they spent on this one.

🐟 Jan: Whhhaaaaaaa. You people are either heartless or blind.

And so it goes. Now if Rhett, Pat, and Wade each figures like Jan that the others have experienced the film somehow incorrectly, then each will merely reinforce his or her own mode of perception with this experience. By realizing and valuing that each person experiences phenomena uniquely, however, these folks might each enrich their own experiences by attempting to perceive in a way additional to the way that feels more immediate or "natural."

You can use what you know[40] of The Medicine Wheel to figure out how you perceive your world. Then you can work to perceive things in ways that don't come as easily to you. Naturally, each of us perceives things in some combination of directions. And those directions change a bit as we change and grow. The idea here is to understand better how you approach situations and then to expand your approach methods. Doing so will enable you to perceive more richly; you will gain knowledge and have more knowledge to use to write persuasively. You might also learn to respect those who might think in ways differently from you.

If everything seems perfectly obvious to you, you might explore things to see why you think of them as you do. If you take everything personally, you might detach for a while and see how others perceive things. If you keep piling up notes and bits of information, you might try to figure out what those notes add up or boil down to. If you've been up on the fourth floor of the library for the last two months, you might try trusting your own perceptions of whatever you've been looking up.

This principle of expanding your cognitive abilities works well in groups of people who "naturally" have differing approaches. In classes teachers sometimes ask students to gather into groups to discuss something or to work together on problems. By discussing ideas with people who approach situations differently from you, you can not only gain from their insights as they gain from you, but you can also watch

---

[40] Which certainly isn't much if this is your only source of information.

how they think. Don't just abandon how your mind works comfortably, but try to expand your cognitive methods—your mind.[41]

As you (or your teacher) form class workshops, you should try to create groups that might generate the richest possible insights. Try, therefore, to form groups of people who (you might guess) think differently from one another. An efficient way to do this is to get together with people who do not look like you. Take a cue from Native Americans' use of various clothing motifs to identify personal characteristics: look at hair. If you are a skinhead, get together with a longhair. If you are a grayhair, get together with a person sporting a multicolored spiked job. If you are a young timid high school completion student, try to get together with an old gnarly looking sage.[42] If you are a slob, look for someone who appears very tidy.

INVENTION EXERCISE #1

In your class, form groups that appear promising in terms of cognitive diversity. (That is, get with people who look alien to you.) Someone in the group then pulls some object out of purse, briefcase, bookbag, backpack. Each student in the group should then write a bit in reaction to the object. Having written a bit in reaction to the object, students then can try to figure out where (what direction) they are each coming from. By determining how each of you approaches objects or phenomena or situations, you might determine how you can expand your approaches. Write about that too.

---

[41] So far this invention strategy is perfectly legal.
[42] If your college or university admits students who all look alike, you are in danger of the clone class and you might alert authorities that you need greater cultural diversity to help you learn new cognitive methods.

INVENTION EXERCISE #2

Take some object or phenomenon or situation and write about it:

- first in terms of its details;
- then in terms of your introspective reaction to it;
- then in terms of what you know or can find out about it;
- finally in terms of some general statement or abstraction about it.

INVENTION EXERCISE #3

Form a group of four students. Settle on something to write about—an idea or situation or object. Each group member then writes from a single different direction of The Medicine Wheel. Having done so, negotiate to put all these various views together into a single piece of writing.[43] This is called "collaborative writing." In the business world this is called "being a team player."

> "If you have a garden and a library,
> you have everything you need."
> ~~Cicero

---

[43] Ah, "two heads are better than one" or "too many cooks spoil the broth"?

© alex74/Shutterstock.com

IV

Arrangement

Or

How to Organize your Materials

"Socrates: No, he doesn't get anywhere near what we're looking for here. He writes backwards—like a person swimming backwards, on his back, upstream, through the current of his own discourse. What he starts out with, he should say at the very end . . . ."[1]

Now that you've gathered lots and lots of materials for your developing essay, you need to organize / position / arrange them in a way that pleases your reader. To avoid writing that appears swimming backwards, on your back, upstream, through the current of your own discourse, you need to consider the needs and expectations of your academic community. Pretty much, that audience needs the comfort of a historically derived social construct.

From the materials you gather for your essay, you need next discover the point on which your piece will rest.[2] You need also discover the arguments that you can devise from your materials to aid your readers. In other words, of all your random information, you need to determine your main focus and the evidence or examples or illustrations that will explain and/or support that main focus. Having discovered (or developed) this focus or thesis, you can begin to arrange your essay. Cicero names six

---

[1] So the character, Socrates, criticizes Lysias's speech in Plato's dialogue, *The Phaedrus*.
[2] Geologists, engineers, mountaineers, (and writer Wallace Stegner) might explain this as "the angle of repose." Your materials need to sit comfortably on some foundation so your essay will hold together as a good solid piece and not fall apart or bury your reader in an avalanche.

parts of a speech or essay, ordering them in a way that enables you to write most convincingly and persuasively:

Cicero's Recommended Order	Aristotle's Recommended Order
exordium, ➔	introduction,
narrative, ➔	narration,
partition, ➔	the proofs,
confirmation, ➔	(more proofs)
refutation, ➔	interrogation,
peroration. ➔	epilogue.

Cicero's recommended order[3] looks quite a bit like the order recommended by Aristotle. And this order pretty much remains the currently accepted order for an academic essay—nothing new under the sun.

The Exordium (or Lead).

"An exordium is a passage which brings the [readers'] minds into a proper condition to receive the rest of the [essay]." Writers can accomplish this by making their readers "well-disposed, attentive, and receptive." How a writer gets their readers to feel "well-disposed, attentive, and receptive" from the very beginning depends on the type of subject and type of readers that the writer is dealing with. Cicero then figures that a writer can get readers into a receptive frame of mind by using two kinds of exordium: the introduction and the insinuation. The introduction uses direct and plain language. The insinuation by "dissimulatione et circumitione" (hey, you translate—

---
[3] *De Inventione*. I. 19.

sounds pretty slimeball to me) "unobtrusively steals into the mind of the auditor."[4] Cicero shows quite clearly how to "pacify the audience" (or readers) by shifting readers' attention from what they hate to what they favor or by concealing your intentions or by saying that the things that displease your readers also displease you. (Dreadful stuff: no wonder rhetoric got its bad name.)

Actually, Cicero gives writers some very specific and workable ideas for leads and/or introductions. He specifically suggests (if appropriate to the subject) a "new topic or a jest"— "one that meets with uproarious applause and shouts of approval." He also suggests "a fable, or a story, or some laughable incident. Or if the seriousness of the occasion denies an opportunity for a jest, it is not disadvantageous to insert something appalling, unheard of, or terrible at the very beginning."[5] At the same time the exordium should be dignified as appropriate to the occasion—here the academic essay and its audience of professors. Cicero then gives us tips of what does not work. "The most obvious faults, which are by all means to be avoided: it should not be general, common, interchangeable, tedious, unconnected, or out of place." These suggestions all work for the academic essay. Remembers that a good lead should "show" something to the reader, not "tell." For more help with leads and a bit of practice, see page 89 of this chapter.

---

[4] Naturally, this approach would make ol' philosophical and moral-oriented Plato just freak. Ah, the changes that can go on in just a couple of hundred years. Like check out the relationship between morality and economics: During Plato's time people scorned those who out of their own self-interest were beginning to use money rather than goods (olives/wine) as a means of exchange. Debtors (like Plato himself at one point) got sold into slavery. Likewise people feared and scorned those might use rhetoric/language with self-interest rather than in the interests of the whole community. Later, as Rome began to deteriorate, money-lending and debt was so acceptable that the interest rate hit 25% (check your VISA bill) and rhetoricians were showing how to steal into others' minds in slimy manners. Ironically, the oh-so-serious, hard-working, utilitarian Romans criticized the old Greeks for being frivolous and couldn't stand their love of music and athletics. Those were the days —
[5] *De Inventione*. I. 25.

The Narrative.

The narrative is an exposition of events that have occurred or should occur or should be taken to heart. You can state any one of three kinds of narratives: one puts forth the whole reason for the dispute. Another digresses from the issue a bit to attack someone, make a comparison or amuse readers. A third sort of narrative puts the issue or events at hand into a fable of sorts or into a historical context or into a fictitious, but plausible kind of analogy. In any of these sorts of narratives, you should be careful to "be brief, clear, and plausible." To be brief, avoid both superfluous facts and words. To be clear, present events one after another as they occurred. To be plausible, present characteristics and reasons for actions that your readers are accustomed to experience in real life.

The Partition.

The partition clarifies your whole essay. Cicero presents two types. In one sort of partition, you can clearly state the issue and fix your readers' attention on the how you perceive the issue or problem. For starters, you can use the word, "should": "We should retain the current zoning." "If you go into the woods today, you should not go alone."[6] The other sort of partition presents your issue along with some hint of how you will proceed to discuss that issue. For example, "We should retain the current zoning for five reasons." "During your four absences from this class you missed plenty." "How do I love you? Let me count the ways." "The greed, aggression, and carelessness of (Politician X, the managerial staff, gophers) have brought disaster to . . . ." In each case the reader has a pretty good idea of what the writer will present and how the writer will proceed: one paragraph about gopher greed, followed by another paragraph about gopher aggression, followed by another paragraph about gopher

---

[6] "The Teddy Bears' Picnic."

carelessness.[7] Do not, in your partition, start talking to your readers;[8] rather, focus your readers' attention on your subject. **Do not** say, "This paper will discuss three ways the US Forest Service can protect mountain goats" or "In this paper I will discuss several ways the US Forest Service can protect mountain goats."[9] **Do** say, "The U.S. Forest Service can protect mountain goats in three ways." That is, your subject is neither "this paper" nor "I." Your subject is the bloomin' Forest Service so make that the subject of your sentence. Subject, get it? That's why it's called "subject." (Review "Chapter 1, How to Write a Thought" to avoid using this tour guide approach).

Confirmation or Proofs.
"Confirmation or proof is the part of the [essay] that by marshaling arguments lends credit, authority, and support to [your writing]."[10] In other words, you start presenting the arguments or proofs, <u>in order</u>, as you promised your reader in your partition. These proofs should lend "credit, authority, and support" to your writing.

So now you should have a number of proofs or illustrations or examples to prove, illustrate, or explain your issue. And you know to put all these proofs after the partition (which goes after the narrative, which goes after the exordium—introduction rather than insinuation, I should hope). Now you have to put these proofs in some order of their own. The theory behind how to arrange the proofs, Cicero says, comes from mixing arrangement with some invention. That is, the arrangement of proofs should lead readers along as if the readers are doing the invention—investigating your issue for themselves. Readers will be comfortable being led through your examples,

---

[7] Here's hoping no biology students are throwing darts at this book.
[8] As I'm doing here.
[9] Some writing instructors call this "the tour guide" approach. Avoid such a condescending tone.
[10] *De Inventione*. I. 34.

illustrations, proofs in a number of ways.[11] In high school you probably learned to put your proofs in any old random order and then stick number signs on them: "First, blah, blah. Second, blah, blah. Next, blah, blah. Finally, blah, blah."—with the "blah, blah" parts having no order of their own. Well, your writing is about to get better; you're going to put some order to your random proofs, illustrations, examples.[12]

Beginning writing classes usually teach students to organize their essays, language-wise, by using words that indicate some order. Unfortunately, the numbers or words had order, but the "proofs" or back-up materials had no order. The coherence (or lack of coherence) of the beginning essay depends on

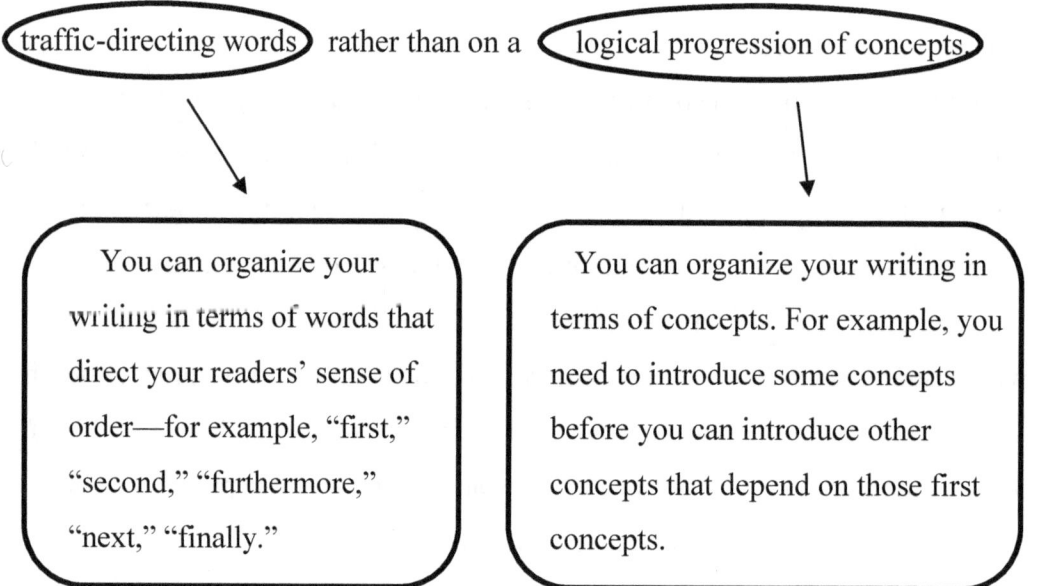

Yes, the old "first, second, finally" business of getting your reader to think that your argument is logical does work, but it's a training wheels strategy at best and

---

[11] See, that sentence is a partition.
[12] At this point Cicero gives us a reasoning method using a dialogue in which Socrates learns some very artistic philosophical and logical persuasion from his mentor, Aspasia. *De Inventione*. I. 51, 52.

misleading at worst. Now might be the time to grow out of it and move on to writing with an actual logical progression of concepts.

Further, within that logical progression of proofs you can create little nesting logical orders. To create a logical order, you can order your proofs by moving from lesser individual pieces of information building up to more general statements of what those pieces of information "add up to." This movement reflects an inductive progression. To explain this arrangement in terms of invention (as Cicero said we would), this order moves from a mouse-like view of details toward some eagle-like generalization or abstraction that logically grows out of those details. Example: "I don't like liver any more. I feel bad eating dead birds. Bovine body parts are gross and my Jewish gramma was right about pork. Gee, I must be turning vegetarian." Cicero adds a couple of tips for this sort of progression: use only truthful analogies and get the reader to buy into the first few examples/proofs without knowing where you're going with those examples/proofs.

You can also order your proofs by moving from a probable conclusion (generalization or abstraction) to the constituent parts that comprise that conclusion. This movement reflects a deductive progression, moving from an eagle-like statement to the mouse-like observations that explain the eagle-like statement. Example: Says Corazon Aquino—"Of course I can run a country; I run a household. Running a household requires a knowledge and experience with finances, internal and external. Running a household requires skill in interpersonal relationships and public relations. Running a household . . . ."[13] Often this sort of reasoning makes "jumps" that do not require explanation. Example: "But I was at Athens on the day of the murder in Rome." Here you do not need to explain that "If I was in Athens of the day on which

---

[13] This is not an accurate quotation, but an embellished historical quotation, fixed up for purposes of illustration.

the murder was committed at Rome, I could not have been present at the murder."
This sort of reasoning, then, draws your readers into your mode of reasoning by letting/making them supply some of the (your) persuasion themselves. That is, deduction gains strength by drawing on community assent. You may note that both of these schemes for ordering proofs seem to embed a mini-order of an essay into the larger essay itself. Determining some order already (seemingly naturally) inherent in your proofs can help you see what order may be more appropriate for presenting those proofs.

The Refutation (or dealing with the anticipated counter-argument).
Like Aristotle's "interrogation," the refutation dispels any problems that you suspect (or know) your reader might have with your take on your issue. You can do this by showing how assumptions basic to an opposing idea are not properly grounded or true. So look at the opposing views and see what assumptions lie there. Cicero also alerts us to look at any "sign" that an opposing view might stand on. Often such signs are just examples (as opposed to foundations) of something. Look also for any objections you might imagine for any ideas introduced as parallel that really are not parallel. For example, using past circumstances to illustrate current situations does not always (or even usually) fit. Look for and diffuse false analogies: "although this situation resembles what happens when we mix A & B, we need to realize blah, blah . . . ." Look for "faulty enumerations" where your reader probably hasn't thought of (or purposely ignores) a circumstance or element of your issue. You can explain (gently) false and far-fetched arguments. Look for bad definitions or how opposing views might offend the sensibilities of your readers. You can point out false assumptions. When trying to persuade your readers of something for which they may have a good strong objection, show that your position is stronger in other respects:

While "we acknowledge that the course of action which they defend is advantageous, ours is more honorable." Or, "while we acknowledge that clear-cutting this acreage may be economically advantageous in the short-term, doing so will leave the region without a future economic base." In current academic writing you can consider the refutation optional. If it seems needlessly aggressive to refute a suspected objection, then leave this part out and accentuate the positive.

The Peroration (or conclusion).
"The peroration is the end and conclusion of the whole [essay]; it has three parts, the summing-up, the *indignatio* or exciting of indignation or ill-will against the opponent, and the *conquestio* or the arousing of pity and sympathy."[14] As you "sum-up" your persuasive essay, try not to repeat so much as to remind your reader of your material. Better yet, try to draw a conclusion that proceeds from your material. In terms of Cicero's *indignatio*, you can turn your readers away from opposing views by citing authorities in your favor,[15] emphasizing who was or will be affected by the situation at hand, pointing out "what would happen if everybody else should act in the same way," that is, what would result from extending the circumstances of your issue, showing the extent of people or other situations affected, showing the irreversible nature of the issue, or its conscious, evil purpose. And Cicero lists many more. Finally, in terms of *conquestio* you can seek to arouse the pity of your readers for your issue. Cicero cautions you not to dwell on this appeal, however, citing the rhetorician Apollonius who said, "Nothing dries more quickly than tears."

---

[14] *De Inventione*. I. 98.
[15] Although Cicero advises otherwise, in current academic writing you'll want to stay away from citing such authorities as "gods, casting of lots, oracles, soothsayers, portents, and prodigies." Given the current distrust in the academic community for "forefathers, kings, states, nations, the senate, and authors of laws," you might want to go easy on them too. Stick to authorities within the field of your subject or acknowledged experts.

WHAT TO DO, HOW TO DO ARRANGEMENT, 1

An Exercise

The next page gives you some pieces from which a writer might develop an essay:

- an exordium (or lead)
- a narrative and partition (or thesis),
- three confirmations (or proofs) (to be put in order, of course!!!),
- a refutation (or dealing with the anticipated counter-argument),
- a peroration (or conclusion).

Note the page is perforated. Tear it out of the book and cut all the sentences apart from one another. Play with these scraps of paper, moving them around to figure out which pieces are appropriate for the lead, for the thesis, for the three proofs—in order, for dealing with the anticipated counter-argument, and for the conclusion. This playing around is called arranging or organizing your essay. When you decide on what you think is the best order, paste or tape them down. Then compare the way you organized these parts to the way other students thought to organize the materials. Discuss your reasons for organizing your essays as you did. There are perfectly good reasons why each piece has a place. There is a right answer! You can even draw a picture of how the three proofs work. After you feel comfortable with such an exercise, you can apply such principles of arrangement to your own writing.

Cut apart the following statements; determine their proper order; paste on the next page, 83. Name the rationale for your order of the proofs. Hint: Hungry??

- Numbers of prey species, such as caribou and moose, fluctuate over periods of decades in response to environmental stressors, such as weather, food availability, and predator impact.

- The wolf "control" programs' assumption that reducing the numbers of predators (wolves) will result in a sustainable increase in the number of prey species has been proven untrue by such examples as the boom and crash nature of deer populations in the North East where humans have killed off the predators.

- The Department of Fish and Wildlife should stop its misguided attempts to "control" the wolf population in order to increase the numbers of caribou and moose available for sport hunting.

- Breaking free from the trap set to serve human needs, the wolf ran strongly, despite its limp, once again demonstrating and obeying nature's directive to live in a complex weave of biotic interactions.

- By radically changing the numbers of prey (moose and caribou) or predators (wolves), humans can disrupt what has evolved as a balanced and dynamic system.

- Gnawing its foot, caught firmly in the iron trap, the half frozen wolf vividly showed the will to roam its native territory.

- The numbers of predators, such as wolves, increase and decrease periodically in response to such environmental factors as food (caribou and moose) availability.

(This page is blank because you are cutting up the back of it, page 81.)

Now order the pieces of the wolf essay. There is, indeed, a correct order. You'll know it, when you get it! Name the rationale of the order.

Exordium (or Lead)

Narrative / Partition (or Thesis)

Confirmation One (or First Proof)

Confirmation Two (or Second Proof)

Confirmation Three (or Third Proof)

Refutation (or Dealing with the Anticipated Counter-Argument)

Peroration (or Conclusion)

What to Do, How to Do Arrangement, 2

Step 1

To write most effectively and most efficiently, forget about writing until you have put lots of energy into the invention and arrangement stages of your essay. With invention, you gathered information about your subject—the more the better. You've exhausted your time, energy, and resources.[16] The information you've gathered does more than just fill in the blanks and provide proofs for your own preconceptions. Your information is more than just stuff that you (in all your big wisdom) manipulate. Your information should now tell you something about what you think. That's why it's called "information"—because it **informs** you as you will use it to inform others. So having used any number of those inventions schemes (in Chapter III) and having gathered lots of materials from primary and secondary (remember the road-trip?) sources, now just ponder it all for a while. Give yourself permission to let all this information you've found inform you.

Step 2

Photocopy any materials that need to remain intact and grab some scissors and cut the photocopied masses of it all apart, idea by idea. On each scrap write down what the source is by author or title or some weird little code of your own. Doing so is important for later citing your sources and creating your Works Cited page. Do not do this cutting up in a windy area. Also, go find some tape.

---

[16] Hawaiian surfers refer to the sweet exhaustion of concluding a wonderful day of surfing as being "all pau."

STEP 3

Now find a roll of paper towels. Or old timey butcher paper. Or some of that computer paper that comes all attached together like a roll of paper towels. Or take some sheets of paper (one side blank) out of a recycling bin and tape some of them all together end to end to make a big long Roman scroll. Or, if in a sunny urban environment with sidewalks and little kids with chalk, take your writing stuff out there (remember to avoid wind).

STEP 4

OK. You're ready to work with arrangement. Look at your assignment or syllabus or wherever it says how long your essay should be. Add a page or two because you'll probably end up taking out "junk" (irrelevant material) as you revise and edit. Now, measure out on your paper towels or computer paper or recycled/taped scroll or sidewalk the physical length of your imagined, completed paper. Measure out about a foot per page plus some—five feet for a four page paper, twelve feet for a ten page paper, and so on.

STEP 5

Look at the stuff you've just read here about arrangement. You're going to map out on your big ol' scroll an arrangement pattern. How long each part of your essay is depends on how long you want your finished essay, but the proportions stay about the same whether you're writing a five-page paper or a 300-page dissertation.[17] So on the edge of your big ol' scroll, write out the parts of your essay:

---

[17] If you are using this textbook to write a 300-page dissertation, the author sends sympathy. Your proportions here will stay the same, but for your own sanity break the project down into 25 page sections or chapters. Then your first chapter will be the exordium, the second will become the narrative, etc.

exordium narrative partition < confirmation > refutation peroration

Of course, your scroll will be much longer (depending on the projected length of your writing). The exordium, narrative, and partition essentially make up your introduction. You begin with your parable or little story or shocking statistics, then get into some narrative discussion of the situation (defining your terms here), and then show your reader where you are going with your issue and your writing. For a five-page essay these parts will be at least a paragraph or two, but not much longer than a page.

Give your proofs, illustrations, examples, at least a paragraph apiece to prove, illustrate, explain your issue. This is the bulk or body[18] of your paper. Most writing teachers now sort of giggle embarrassedly remembering the old 5-paragraph essay. You may have more or fewer than three proofs. I'm not going to tell you how many paragraphs or proofs you need/want/put here because I don't know what you are writing about. Just make sure you communicate effectively (not too long, not too short, but just right) for good friendly persuasion.

Finally, (perhaps, this is optional) address any problems you suspect your reader may have with your proposal and then conclude in a paragraph or two.

STEP 6

When you have your scroll all partitioned out, spread all your bits (bytes?) of information out and figure out where each piece goes. Move things around. Reconsider. Move things around again. When you get your information arranged just how it best can lead a reader through your issue and to your conclusion, grab the tape and tape the pieces down. You should end up with something looking like a long

---

[18] All these human (and male) metaphors we use for writing come from the Greek love of the human form. Since (to the ancient Greeks) the human form is the most wonderful model of anything there is, then the arts (including the art of rhetoric) should celebrate it. So you can't say "on the other hand" without first saying "on the one hand" and we still speak of the body of the paper, having ideas well grounded, etc.

paper fringed scarf and tape/glue all over your hands. So that's invention and arrangement.

STEP 7

Sit down at a keyboard with your scroll by your side and write it all up as fast and mindlessly as you can. Don't get hung up on the words. Your scroll prevents that now obsolete disease writer's block.[19] With your scroll right there in your face, you can do no wrong. You're guaranteed to write a brilliantly informed and beautifully organized essay.

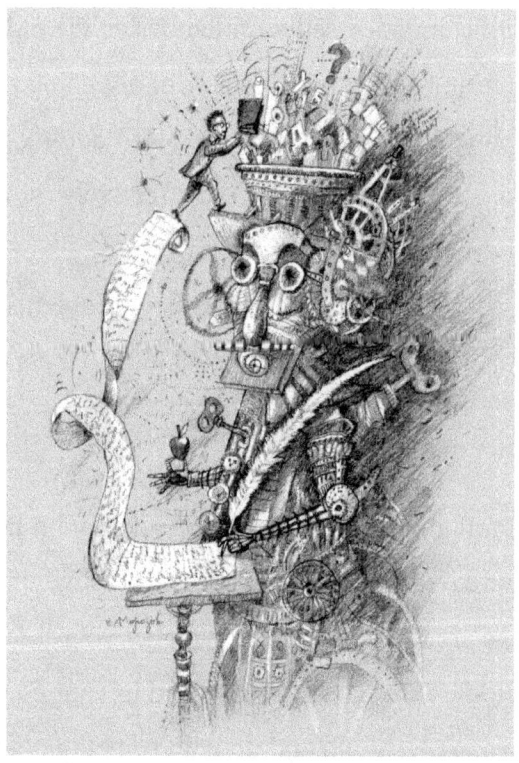

© alex74/Shutterstock.com

---

[19] Disease caused by the impossible situation of having to write something without any clue of what to write or what to put where. Cicero's method of dealing with invention and arrangement <u>before even thinking about actually writing</u> completely cures this now obsolete (if you are reading this) disease.

WHAT TO DO, HOW TO DO ARRANGEMENT, 3
A WORD (OR SEVERAL) ABOUT LEADS

Again, a good lead should put your readers' "minds into a proper condition to receive the rest of the [essay]." Writers can accomplish this by making their readers "well-disposed, attentive, and receptive."[20] Actually, Cicero gives writers some very specific and workable ideas for leads and/or introductions. He specifically suggests (if appropriate to the subject) a "new topic or a jest." He also suggests "a fable, or a story, or some laughable incident. Or if the seriousness of the occasion denies an opportunity for a jest, it is not disadvantageous to insert something appalling, unheard of, or terrible at the very beginning." Cicero then gives us tips of what does not work. Leads "should not be general, common, interchangeable, tedious, unconnected, or out of place." These suggestions all work for the academic essay. Remembers that a good lead should "show" something to the reader, not "tell."

Often students begin with leads that Cicero says don't work: general, common, tedious, out of place, etc.

- Avoid the condescending question: "Have you ever thought about blah, blah, blah?" (Yuck.)
- Avoid the Webster's (or Wikipedia) definition: "Webster's defines love as . . . . ." (Yuck.)
- Avoid the ordering your professors around:[21] "Just imagine . . . ." "Think about . . . ." (Yuck.)
- Avoid the media-talk of one word/image, period, fragment: "Aging. Not for sissies." "Bungee jumping. The thrill of your life." (Yuck.)

---

[20] Cicero gives the impression that in your lead you should pretty much consciously and overtly take charge of your readers' minds. (Heavy handed?)
[21] See the section on "Imperative Voice," near the end of "Chapter 5, Style."

- Avoid the "tour guide": "This essay will begin by blah, blah, and then explain blah, blah, and then we'll all have cookies." (Yuck.)

Instead, begin with an anecdote, fable, story, description of a scene or mood or incident. The easiest way is to skim your first draft and find such an anecdote. Chances are that you've put some anecdote in somewhere as an example of something or other. Just pull that little story out and use it for a lead. Be sure to fix up the hole you left by pulling it out.

If you can't find some anecdote that you've already written, come up with a relevant story or scene or weird statistic. Advice: Plato (and I) advise you to make your lead sound as if it really happened by using the past tense. The media has probably has probably given you the inclination to use the present tense: Resist. Some students find themselves so impacted by the media's ploy to make things sound "right now" that they do a weird time travel that mixes present and past. For example, "Last Thursday, Fred and I walk down Broadway." Resist and tell your story as if it actually happened last Thursday: "Last Thursday, Fred and I walk<u>ed</u> down . . . ." Plato says that the hypothetical incident or story lacks the credibility of the (apparently) real incident. Don't fall into the trap of sounding like a screen play or sports announcer. Avoid "Sally goes to class every day without a decent breakfast. She sits dazed through arithmetic until she finally gets some milk and graham crackers." Instead, make this situation real with some specifics and past tense: "When she was in the fourth grade, Sally went to class every day without a decent breakfast. She sat dazed through arithmetic until she finally got some milk and graham crackers."

Importantly, make your lead "show, not tell." Don't <u>tell</u> "there was a big bar room brawl." Instead, <u>show</u> that brawl: "Rocky Raccoon checked into his room, only to find Gideon's Bible. Rocky had come, equipped with a gun, to shoot off the legs of his rival." Don't <u>tell</u>, "Clear cutting the forest on Mt. Hood makes me sick." Instead, <u>show</u> that clear cutting makes you sick: "Exhilarated from our six-hour hike through the meadows and bogs of Mt. Hood, we followed the foot-path into the forest to climb to the overlook for lunch. Abruptly, we found ourselves in the dust and desolation of twisted branches and upturned roots that extended as far as we could see. A frightened fawn looked for her mother." Get the picture?

© Alexandra Giese/Shutterstock.com

Now it's your turn to work with these principles. Change these weak <u>telling</u> "leads" to interesting scenes, stories, anecdotes that <u>show</u>. Be sure to keep them in the past tense.

1. Have you ever wondered why kids in the city get scared when they go camping and see stars for the first time?

   _____
   _____
   _____
   _____

2. The traffic in Portland, OR, is outrageous.

   _____
   _____
   _____
   _____

3. My teachers are very strange.

   _____
   _____
   _____
   _____

4. My new puppy is so cute.

5. College demands are overwhelming.

6. Public transportation. What a trip.

7. This essay will explain all the gruesome diseases that can happen to you if you do not floss.

_____
_____
_____
_____

8. Courtney has a lot of trouble writing leads.

_____
_____
_____
_____

Now that you know how to write leads, you're ahead of the game when it comes to the next chapter:

STYLE.[22]

_____

[22] For regular old Standard English tips, see the rather comical website, The Oatmeal: http://theoatmeal.com/tag/grammar

V
STYLE
OR
DON'T PUT BIG WORDS IN; JUST TAKE THE LITTLE ONES OUT

Cicero opens *De Optimo Genere Oratorum* with a brief sketch of the ideal orator (or for our purposes—writer) that reviews some of the rhetorical tips you've learned:

> Ideal [writers] should instruct, delight, and move their readers. Their diction should be pure and flawless, their words decorous and appropriate. . . . They will arrange their ideas in the best way, and they will know the principles of memory and delivery. In short, perfect writers are supreme in managing the five canons of oratory.[1]

And gaining this "supremacy" ain't easy:

> Whether [speaking or writing] is a product of rules and theory, or a technique dependent on practice, or on natural gifts, it is one attainment among all others of unique difficulty. For of the five elements of which, as we say, it is made up, each one is in its own right a great art. One may guess therefore what power is inherent in an art made up of five great arts, and what difficulty it presents.[2]

In order to do all these things, as Cicero repeatedly emphasizes, successful speakers and writers must first know what they are talking about:

> No one can be a good speaker [or writer] who is not a sound thinker.[3]

---

[1] Quiz: Name the five canons of oratory (how do you go about writing?) (Hint: name chapters 3-7.)
You are now about to encounter the third of the canon.
　　①invention　②arrangement　③style　④memory　⑤delivery

[2] *Brutus*. VI. 25.

[3] *Brutus*. VI. 23.

> [Wannabe speakers/writers] demonstrate a gross lack of tact when they plunge into a discussion on any subject regardless of their knowledge on the topic.[4] True eloquence depends on a wide knowledge of philosophy, psychology, sociology, and politics. I suggest, therefore, that our [writer] study well the teaching of both the old and new Academies. . . . Eloquence, properly understood, encompasses nearly all knowledge, especially knowledge of human behavior. . . . [A writer], therefore, must have a wide educational background drawn either from philosophy or from experience.[5]

Having based good speaking/writing on a speaker/writer's knowledge, Cicero then moves to language. Your success at writing depends on an intermingling of both knowledge and your actual use of words.

> Every [essay] consists of substantive matter and words. Each depends on the other in much the same way that nothing in the universe is self-sufficient. No matter the subject or goal of any essay, it must consist of matter and form, and . . . neither can be separated except in the abstract.[6]

Cicero actually defines what it is to be a good speaker/writer by how well such a person can combine knowledge and language:

> I define orators [writers], therefore, as people who can speak in such a way that they persuade listeners [readers]. To accomplish this end, writers must immerse themselves in public affairs and practice the art continuously.[7]

That is,

> The orator [writer] must learn to speak skillfully on subjects involving society, politics, psychology, and morals.[8]

---

[4] *De Oratore*. II. 17. Like politicians bought off by oil interests?
[5] *De Oratore*. III. 70 & 80.
[6] *De Oratore*. III. 20.
[7] *De Oratore*. I. 260.

And having gathered such knowledge and materials,

> [Our ideal speakers\writers] will use this stock intelligently, and weigh everything and select. . . . They will exercise judgment, and will not only discover something to say, but will estimate its value. . . . They will set the results of invention in order with great care. They will make good honest porches[9] and gorgeous approaches to the essay. And having gained attention by the introduction, [ideal speakers\writers] will establish a case, [present appropriate examples\illustrations\proofs], refute any opposing views, [and conclude]. . . .

When speakers have discovered what to say and how to arrange their subject-matter, then comes the all-important question of the manner of presentation.[10] And so, you have combined what you have done with invention and arrangement on a length of paper towels and have tapped the first draft into the machine—writing on yellow tablets permitted too. Now you move to fixing up that first draft by messing with the language. Onward to some ancient and currently fashionable principles of style. Just remember, though:

> The unique trait of good speakers [writers] is their embellishment, distinct, and arranged presentation, in other words, their style. Yet style without substance is ludicrous.[11]

Here come some observations from Cicero and then some tips for more current style.

---

[8] *De Oratore*. II. 65.
[9] A metaphor: the introduction as an inviting porch or entrance to your essay. Come on in.
[10] *Orator*. IV. 50-51.
[11] *De Oratore*. I. 50.

Cicero observes and tells us of three kinds of style: the grand, the plain, and a style in between those two extremes—the tempered. Cicero characterizes the grand style as that popularized by the Sophists—tricky slick talkers who for their own personal gain used all sorts of language craftiness to hood-wink listeners. Speakers and writers who use grand style can be forceful, versatile, copious, and grave. With training to "arouse and sway the emotions,"[12] writers can learn to write with such force. Consider, for example, commercials and the training of those who write them. Do pop-ups appeal to your sense of logic? How do advertisers create desire? And what is the motive for creating desire? Cicero feared that using language for self-interest rather for the good of the community might cause the community to deteriorate. This was shortly before the fall of the Roman Empire.[13]

Perhaps you observe that academic discourse style differs somehow from the discourse style of a blaring advertisement. Admittedly, the grand style can show a "splendid power of thought and majesty of diction" and such artistry is a good thing. The problem comes with motive. When, as a writer, you get the sense that you are choosing words and sentence structures to point the reader toward you as author rather than choosing words to communicate most clearly for the good of your readers, reconsider. In short, don't use big words to make yourself look cool. Your academic readers easily spot posers and find them a source of amusement. As Cicero says, "It is easy, indeed, to criticize some flaming word, if I may use this expression, and to laugh at it when the passion of the moment has cooled."[14]

Whereas the grand style appeals to the passions, the plain style appeals proportionately more to your readers' sense of logic. Plain style is "to the point, explaining everything and making every point clear rather than impressive, using a

---

[12] *Orator*. V. 20.
[13] Consider this aspect of language use before the next election.
[14] *Orator*. VIII. 27. "Flaming,"—appeals to the passions, did not begin with the internet.

refined, concise style stripped of ornament." Despite the apparent "dryness" of this style, you can work to make your academic writing "neater, elegant, even brilliant and to a slight degree ornate."[15] Cicero challenges his readers to produce some discourse that is at once both "ornate and weighty, and also shrewd and plain."

Ideas of what is "ornate" and what is "plain" fluctuate with history and fashion. In terms of classical rhetoric, ornate writing was sometimes accused of "Asianisms"—Asia at that time being more in the sense of Turkey and Persia than how we more recently think of Asia. Some rhetoricians explain cultural styles in terms of art and architecture. The Greeks perceived Turkish and Persian architecture as strong structures with decorations applied on the surface of those structures—like tiled mosaics or paintings. In contrast, the Greeks perceived their own architecture as beautiful in and of its own structures without need of *applied* ornamentation. Its beauty was in its plain and evidenced strength. These ideas of beauty in human creations went for language as well as building and since our discourse methods derive largely from Greek ideas, we still consider language likewise. American turn-of-the-century (1800 to 1900) rhetorician Gertrude Buck (whom you met in Chapter 1) explains that writers create less effective metaphors by gluing them onto a piece of writing as ornament. Writers create more effective metaphors by thinking in imagery. Do not paste big and fancy words onto your thoughts and into your writing. If some thought comes to you as a metaphor or image and you can communicate your idea most effectively to your readers as that image, go ahead. Do not write with "high ambition, but poor judgment"; rather, use eloquence to achieve quiet strength in your writing.

---

[15] *Orator*. VI. 20.

As a determining principle, remember your readers. A writer's height of eloquence—from grand to plain—

> has always been controlled by the good sense of the audience, since all who desire to win approval have regard to the goodwill of their [readers,] and shape and adapt themselves completely according to this and to their opinion and approval.[16]

Note that the current governmental plea for their agencies and American professions to use "plain English" has less to do with the traditional sense of plain vs. ornate and more to do with the current sense of plain vs. incomprehensible. By applying all you learn here to your writing, you will be in healthy compliance with the government call.

One more Ciceronian tip regarding your readers comes across as a veiled warning—readers don't appreciate or even notice good style when it exists, but quickly dismiss a writer's ideas when good style is missing.

> Most of an oration's [essay's] power comes from its style. Instinctively, it seems, people can discriminate and evaluate whatever is applied to their senses. Few [readers] understand the nature of balanced, rhythmic [discourse], but nearly all can detect a blemish.[17]

> Any blemish or error in an orator [writer] is immediately apparent. We demand total perfection in any person whom we designate as eloquent.[18]

Quite a threat.

Cicero finally gets around to giving us some specific instructions. In public writing or speaking, writers should slightly increase the use of vocabulary and allow a somewhat greater freedom in rhythm and sentence structure. Public speaking/writing

---

[16] *Orator*. VIII. 24.
[17] *De Oratore*. III. 195.
[18] *De Oratore*. I. 130.

allows you to indulge in a neatness and symmetry of sentence and use well rounded periods. In this sort of writing you may measure your words in equal length phrases and pair your ideas together, as, for example, in Kennedy's famous "ask not what the country can do for you; ask what you can do for your country" or, Seale's "you're either part of the problem or part of the solution." Also, as in writing song lyrics, you can have clauses end the same way or with similar sounds. Poets, Cicero observes, can pay more attention to sound than to sense. In a courtroom or legislative chamber, you can't indulge in such obvious word play. If, as decision-makers, readers notice you appealing to their sense of aesthetics rather than "just the facts, Ma'am," they might just throw out your ideas along with your language. Yet, later Cicero characterizes successful language in court or in legislative situations as that able

> to prove, to please, and to sway or persuade. To prove is the first necessity, to please is charm, to sway is victory. . . . For these three types of writing there are three styles, the plain style for proof, the middle style for pleasure, and the vigorous style for persuasion. . . . Writers who control and combine these three varied styles need rare judgment and great endowment[19] to decide what is needed at any point. . . . For after all the foundation of eloquence, as of everything else, is wisdom. In writing, as in life, nothing is harder than to determine what is appropriate. . . . Writers must have an eye to propriety not only in thought but in language. . . . The universal rule, in writing as in life, is to consider propriety. This depends on the subject under discussion, and on the character of both the writer and the reader. . . . "Propriety" is what is fitting and agreeable to an occasion or person. It is important often in actions as well as in words.

---

[19] Of mind.

Cicero points out that the plain style of academic discourse is not just inept or simple to learn, but probably the most difficult style to attempt. Without obvious ornamentation, plain style writing should still "have some of the sap of life." Without obvious rhythms, "it should be loose, but not rambling." You should try to use what are called "periodic" structures. That is, end your sentences and paragraphs with some pizzazz—at least a noun. The idea of the periodic structure gives us the punch line. You make things clear at the end of the sentence rather than at the beginning to create some impact. For example, "if I were in a better mood and if I were as hungry as I was yesterday, and if . . . blah, blah, blah, but I'm not, so forget it." You can feel a certain directness to this structure, which should make communication quite plain. Cicero likens the strength of the plain style to women's appearances.[20]

> Just as some women are said to be handsomer when unadorned—this very lack of ornament becomes them—so this plain style gives pleasure even when unembellished: there is something in both cases which lends greater charm, but without showing itself.[21]

In short, to develop a plain, elegant, academic style, you should

> not be bold in coining words, and in metaphor be modest, spare the out-dated phrases, and remain somewhat subdued in using the other embellishments of language and of thought. . . . Use metaphors that make sense to your readers, not those that might seem far-fetched.[22]

Interestingly, twenty-first-century style fairly closely follows these principles.

---

[20] So what's new?

[21] *Orator*. XXIII. 76-79. Cicero continues,
> Also all noticeable ornaments, pearls as it were, will be excluded; not even curling-irons will be used; all cosmetics, artificial white and red, will be rejected; only elegance and neatness will remain.

That's a metaphor.

[22] *Orator*. XXV. 82.

INTERLUDE # 1

Before we get to tips for late twentieth- and early twenty-first century style, we need some remarks regarding grammar. Many people and writing students currently conflate (mix up by putting together) grammar and style. Yes, the academic essay does call for the grammar of some strange dialect called "Standard English." This dialect is *so* strange that it's the only dialect in our language that does not grow organically out of some situation, but has to be taught—in schools, which is about the only place that it's ever used. This circumstance is rather odd, linguistically.

Now there are various ways to consider grammar. The current sense of grammar is as a bunch of rules with value judgments of "good" and "bad" attached. This view of grammar brings with it indicators of class and smartness or stupidity. Another view of grammar is the older view—way old. Once upon a time grammar was one of the big three ways of knowing: The Trivium. The trivium comprised logic, rhetoric, and grammar as ways of determining knowledge.[23] That is, in the very old days people used grammar as a means of inquiry—a way of figuring things out. By thinking of grammar in this old way we gain an incredibly powerful new tool for communication. By listening for a person's (or institution's) grammatical structures, you can perceive whether that person or institution is being friendly or is intending to exploit or coerce you. Institutional forms and letters (they call them "notices"), for example, often use what is called passive voice to make them seem big and you feel little. More on this trick later. Or, for example, we can look at gender use through the lens of grammar and learn why despite all the apparent and legislated equality of the

---

[23] The knowledge itself comprised what was known as the Quadrivium: namely, astronomy, mathematics, arithmetic, and music. Notice how all these aspects of knowledge interplay—the music of the stars; divide an instrument string geometrically in half and you get an octave higher; etc.

sexes women still choose those low paying vocations (like schoolmarm) and men become movers and shakers. Gee, maybe this situation comes embedded in the history and vibes of our language. For example, in Latin the word for the sort of nice smooth, undulating stone that people walk on in the garden is feminine; the word for the kind of rock that is so sharp and hard it can cut a person is "lapis": yup, you guessed it—masculine. More on this sort of thing later too.

So we can use grammar beyond the sense of a bunch of rules with right and wrong or good and bad overtones to learn something of the language that creates the hidden reality we are stuck using to communicate and also to learn something of our own sense of self(s). Keep this principle[24] in mind as we look at the grammatical structures that fade fashionably in and out of style.

INTERLUDE #2—REGARDING GRAMMAR AND CHILD-RAISING

You may note that "kids just ain't how they usta be; no respect." Perhaps a quick look at recent grammatical structures can be instructive. Traditionally, parents and teachers have felt comfortable using directives with children such as "go brush your teeth" or "drink your milk." Then when the child, comfortable with such parental directives, reached sixteen and heard, "be in at ten p.m.," the teenager might have silently grumbled, but did not freak out. Some recent new fangled self-esteem building techniques of child-raising have included less directive grammatical structures—like

---

[24] Note, for example, the use of the term "INTERLUDE." Editor and author went round and round to come up with a term appropriate to both text and audience here. Grammatically, "interlude" is a noun—a fairly harmless thing—and refers to "a short farcical entertainment performed between the acts of a play." The term, "TIME OUT," comes across as imperative—too much of an authoritative order with sports overtones. I could just about hear some dictatorial referee yelling this verb form at my readers. Or a reader could envision some exasperated day-care person yelling "TIME OUT" at a bunch of two-year-olds. Get the connection between grammatical structures and communication?

the statement of fact, "it's time to brush your teeth" or the empowering, "would you like to drink your milk in a red cup or a blue cup"? Now, consider what happens when this child, raised with statements and empowering grammatical structures, hits sixteen and the parent feels the need to use a directive: "be in at ten p.m." Having encountered an unfamiliar dictatorial grammatical structure, the sixteen year old quite accurately feels the affront to sense of self and justifiably freaks out—either internally and repressed to be released later or in a reciprocal grammatical directive like, "get lost." Because of age and tradition, the parent feels justified in the switch of grammatical structures and calls that switch "hard love." The maturing child recognizes the switch of grammatical structures and points to the inconsistency. Inconsistency of grammatical structures causes problems in communication that can blossom as problems in behavior. Both the parent and the child feel the need to resort to behavior that each feels uncomfortable with. The solution remains quite simple—be consistent in your grammatical structures unless you want to upset communication and someone's sense of self. If you'd like to say, "please be back at ten" to your teenager, begin when the child is two by saying "please brush your teeth." If you choose the more modern style of offering self-empowering choices to a two-year old, be prepared to offer those choices to the teenager: "would you prefer to go to school or would you prefer to go surfing in Kauai?" All this business just demonstrates the power of grammatical structures in our communication. Just as the lyrics of songs work with melodic and rhythmic structures, the content of words works with grammatical structures. Just as we communicate with instrumentals as well as with lyrics, we often communicate with grammar as well as with word-meanings. Do consider grammar beyond its sense as a bunch of rules to use it as a very powerful tool of perception and communication.

> **A WORD FROM ALDOUS HUXLEY**
>
> Most of our mistakes are fundamentally grammatical. We create our own difficulties by employing an inadequate language to describe facts. Thus, to take one example, we are constantly giving the same name to more than one thing, and more than one name to the same thing. The results, when we come to argue, are deplorable. For we are using a language which does not adequately describe the things about which we are arguing.
>
> —From *The Elder Peter Bruegel* (1938)

You can communicate more effectively by developing an awareness of certain grammatical structures. The following section will give you specific tips to make your academic style more clear:

- **Use language to communicate rather than to impress;**
- **Arrange your sentences with subject and verb close together;**
- **Focus on agents—whoever does something in your ideas; that is, make the subjects in your head the subjects of your sentences;**
- **Use "plain English";**
- **Take the little words out.**

> We interrupt this chapter for a test of your grammatical broadcasting system. Punctuate this sentence, using commas—or not:
>
> "Woman without her man is nothing."   (Ha!)

Twenty-First-Century Style

Style Principle Number One

Use language to communicate rather than to impress.
Often we try to assume a voice of authority. Unfortunately, sometimes we try to build authority on "how we sound" rather than on the strength of a concept or on our expertise in an area. Usually, relying on language rather than on the concepts carried by language makes us sound "full of hot air." To avoid sounding like a big blow, we often need to concentrate less on self-expression and more on communication.

To protect your psyche from incoming language that might rely on "the big blow," you can use this principle in reverse. When speakers feel inadequate, they often rely on the sound of their own voices rather than on their ideas to impress you. Watch for language that tells you a speaker or writer cares more for self-image than for effecting communication. And watch your own language lest you let someone push you against a wall, scrapping for substance and finding only fluff.

© Katyau/Shutterstock.com

STYLE PRINCIPLE NUMBER TWO

Arrange sentences with subject and verb close together to look like this:

Blah, blah, blah, subject, verb, blah, blah, blah.

For example:

One more wise-crack and I'll punch your lights out, big time.

    blah, blah   subject verb   blah   emphasis

Brilliant economic scholar, Joe Blow demonstrates how blah, blah.

By smacking your subject and verb right next to each other, you can eliminate a lot of confusion in your writing. You especially want to put all the introductory stuff in front of a person's name or in front of some weird word or in front of using "I" so that the introductory stuff hits your reader's brain before what would otherwise seem like generic names or some mind-boggling concepts. If you put a subject first and then a bunch of modifiers for a couple of lines, your reader can't remember what you were talking about and might have to go back and look. If your reader is impatient, you no longer have a reader. For example:

Needlessly stretches the reader:

Ezekiel Plumpkin, brilliant nineteenth-century scholar of the science of the lumpy head, privileges the pointy head.

More clear:

Brilliant nineteenth-century scholar of the science of the lumpy head, Ezekiel Plumpkin privileges the pointy head.

Needlessly stretches the reader:

Vasoconstrictors, those agents in yummy drinks that constrict our blood vessels, have received some questionable press lately. (Huh, what were those things?)

More clear:

Those agents in yummy drinks that constrict our blood vessels, vasoconstrictors, have received some questionable press lately.

Be sure to put some description in front of "I" or "we" or else the "I" appears as just some generic nobody and your readers pay no attention to you or your ideas.

Weak:

I advise you to get a Chevy.   (yeah, sez who?)

Stronger:

Having trashed the brass synchros in two Saab transmissions, I advise you to get a Chevy.

Likewise, define "we" <u>before</u> you use it:

As writing instructors, we should provide students with good solid tips for writing instruction.

Many students have encountered writing teachers who have taught them not to use "I" or "we." You now have a twist on that "rule": use "I" or "we" only to your advantage—by sticking some credibility identifier out in front.

STYLE PRINCIPLE NUMBER THREE

Focus on agents—whoever or whatever does something in your ideas.

That is, make the subjects in your head the subjects of your sentences.

Maybe, as a writer, you've also learned to focus on things rather than on people because focusing on things seems more "objective" and "scientific" whereas focusing on people seems more "subjective"—and everyone knows that appearing more scientific brings more credibility than appearing more subjective. (Ahem. We now question this assumption.) Unfortunately, the effort to remove people from your ideas breeds a whole mess of language problems. For example, consider the following sentences:

- Reading your essay, several questions came to mind.
- Driving down the road, a tree got in my way.
- Taking a writing course, communication is getting easier.
- Scratching his fleas, the rug has now become a bug-haven thanks to our new puppy, Bruno.

A rule-bound sort of grammarian might call all these sentences "bad": dangling participles—ooowheee. The grammarian might explain that those "---ing" phrases are called participles and modify the word that comes next to them. So "several issues" cannot read an essay; a tree cannot drive down the road; communication cannot take a writing course; a rug cannot scratch its fleas. Another sort of grammarian would agree that these sentences do not communicate as effectively as they could if the writer had focused on the person or agent doing whatever is going on. As a writer, you need to figure out who you are talking about. Then put the subject of your concept into the grammatical subject place of your sentence. Again, review Buck's method of writing thoughts: This is why the subject of a sentence is called the subject of the sentence. That is, say who is doing something in the following sentence:

- Reading your essay, several questions came to mind.

Can't figure it out?   Hummmm. Say who is doing something in this second example:

- Driving down the road, a tree got in my way.

Easy: **I** was driving down the road. So to focus on someone doing something here, you could rewrite by putting the subject of your thought into the grammatical subject place:

- I was driving down the road and plowed into a tree.
- Driving down the road, I ran into a tree.
- I found a tree in my way as I drove down the road.

In each of these re-write sentences, the writer puts a person ("I") in the subject place. Yes, you may sound subjective to have "I" as your subject, but what's so objective and scientific about a tree that drives?

Same deal with that apparently more difficult first sentence:

- Reading your essay, several questions came to mind.

Figure out who read that essay. The reader could again be "I" or someone whom you might name, like Dr. Smith. The idea here is clean, honest communication. <u>Communicate</u> who read that essay by putting that person in the subject place:

- Reading your essay, Dr. Smith had several questions.
- I had several questions while reading your essay.

Likewise, clarify

- Taking a writing course, communication is getting easier.

Simple.[25] Just say who is taking the writing course. Who is the unspoken subject of this thought?

- Taking the writing course, Joey found communication getting easier.
- I found communication getting easier as I proceeded through the writing course.

---

[25] "Writing seems much simpler to me in theory." —student, Phaedra Paulson.

Now who is doing what with Bruno and his fleas?

- Scratching his fleas, the rug has now become a bug-haven thanks to our new puppy, Bruno.

To clarify, focus your reader's attention on Bruno, the flea-scratcher:

- By scratching his fleas, our new puppy Bruno has turned our rug into a bug-haven.
- Our new puppy Bruno has scratched a good number of his fleas into our rug which now resembles a bug-haven.

Focusing on agents or making the subject of your thought the subject of your sentence can save you from other communication problems too. For example, consider the subject-verb snafus in the following:

- Running, biking, and cutting back on my chocolate intake helps get me ready for snowboarding.
- Your fall semester grades from the Malibu Sunbathing Institute have been reviewed by our counselors.

By putting some human in the grammatical subject place, you can easily avoid these problems. Just figure out who you're talking about. In the first sentence, the "my" tips you off to who is in the writer's mind: namely, the writer. So put the mental subject into the grammatical subject place and you have:

- I run, bike, and cut back on my chocolate intake to get ready for snowboarding.

In the second example, you need to ask yourself who reviews transcripts around here. Who are you talking about, anyway? Ah, the counselors!

- Our counselors have reviewed your fall semester grades from the Malibu Sunbathing Institute.

Presto: subject-verb agreement problems disappear and your writing becomes much more clear. This tip of writing what you have in mind as the subject of your sentence can help you avoid strange and unwanted uses of the passive voice as well. You'll get a good dose of that in a few pages. All this business means to make lousy writing better. Remember "Chapter I, How to Write a Thought"? By writing using Gertrude Buck's method, you can avoid the later need to "fix" or clarify language.

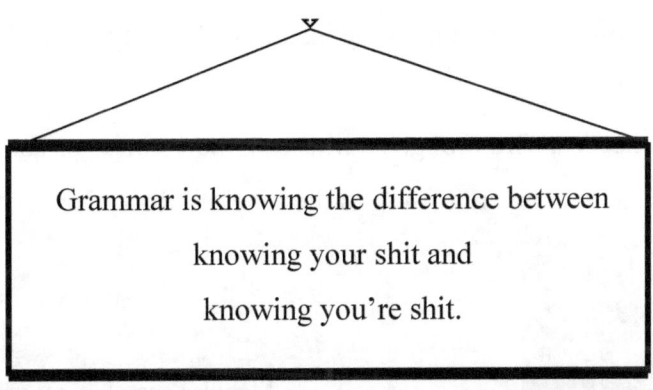

STYLE PRINCIPLE NUMBER FOUR
Avoid using big words just to show off.
As Cicero advises, **never add "big" words just to make yourself seem smart**—chances are, you'll make yourself look like a pretentious idiot and just get chuckles from your teachers. A big word is any word that feels "big" to you. This can be a little word, like "ilk." If a word feels "big" to you, try using a word that feels more comfortable. If all words feel "big" to you, start reading a few hours each day until you feel more comfortable with a greater number of words. Then there won't be as many "big" words in your life.

Be sure to get rid of "big" words that are trendy—like "plethora" or "pertains to" or "preponderance."[26] While you're at it, get rid of stuffy-sounding pseudo-academic filler like, "From all we have looked at in this paper, we can now conclude that . . . ." Or "in this paper we will explore . . . ." Or "with respect to" or "it may be sufficient to observe" or "it has already been observed" or "it is from a consideration of all these circumstances that we are enabled to form a right judgment as to the facts which . . . ."[27] Explaining why such once acceptable language now curls the reading eye-balls of your professors requires some history of language fashion: hang on.

Every text book needs a sing-along. To illustrate the silliness of using big words to show off, please take a moment to sing to the tune of "Row, Row, Row Your Boat":

© Everett Historical/Shutterstock.com

A SING-ALONG!
♫♪

Mobilize, mobilize, mobilize thy skiff,

Languorously down the prevailing effluvium,

Blithesomely, blithesomely,
blithesomely, blithesomely,

Vitality is but a phantasmagoria!
♫♪

(With thanks to collaborator, Dr. Kristin Bryant
and to pianist, James Beaton,
and chanteuse, Storm Large,
who always include a sing-a-long!)

---

[26] As a principle, don't use words that you have learned from a list of impressive words. Do use words (and maybe those same words) that you have incorporated into your thinking and usage from listening and reading. [Thanks to Don Stone who provided me with such a list of pretentious words.]

[27] These last few examples come from eighteenth-century rhetorician Richard Whately.

HISTORICAL INTERLUDE
MOVING FROM NOUNS TO VERBS

That element of culture called "language" grows and changes just as culture itself grows and changes. Sometimes language gets ahead of culture and pulls the culture along. For example, "street language" and "jive talk" have at times entered the language of the dominant culture and altered the ways that people "away from the streets" think and communicate. For example, an accountant might complain that "these figures don't jive," using a word and concept that originated far away from the banking community.

Currently, academic, business, and technical writing often falls about a full generation behind the times. Vocabulary may describe and reflect current circumstances, but grammatical structures that writers use come right out of the 1950s. This time-warp between vocabulary and grammatical structures can cause confusion, miscommunication, and some real embarrassment.

About the '50s.

In the 1950s objects were heavier than we know them today. Large and heavy automobiles had great big tail-fins. Women's bodies had fleshy weight—Marilyn Monroe, Jayne Mansfield, and Carol Doda became famous for their flesh. Clothes were heavy: long circular skirts had padded fuzzy poodles on them. With the cold-war giving people a heavy feeling, some

© Radoslaw Lecyk/Shutterstock.com

people even had very heavy concrete fall-out shelters in their backyards. From televisions to early computers, the "best" appliances were the biggest.[28] With everything being so heavy, people did not move around much. Then President Kennedy initiated a major paradigm shift with a football. By throwing a football around on the White House lawn, Kennedy astonished the country with the concept that people could function actively. The President's Council on Physical Fitness expanded to have poor unsuspecting school kids urged (by big heavy physical education teachers) to run around a track for the first time in their lives. The cultural identity move from sedentary to active continued and intensified. Currently, our culture favors spiffy little fast-moving sport cars to the tanks of the '50s, anorexic fashion models, and computers that have shrunk from luggable to laptop to notebook to nano. And guess what: language has changed in much the same way.

    Language of the '50s used to be full of very heavy object-words: nouns. More current language favors action-words: verbs. This situation creates an unfortunate snare for academic, business, and technical writers. Most people read books written by authors who learned to write in the 1950s; perhaps you learned to write from teachers educated in the 1950s.[29] No wonder, then, that written academic and business language often sounds as bulky and awkward as an old Studebaker. The challenge becomes fairly apparent: we need to get rid of the heavy fat to make our writing more active and dynamic. This is about as easy as losing all the weight you've

---

[28] That biggest is best has fallen by the economic wayside. See Bill McKibben's *Deep Economy*.
[29] Or perhaps you weren't taught how to write at all. I recall being told to write with no instruction and then facing a returned paper covered with red ink pointing out all the bad things I had done. Those were the days when grammar was more important than communication.

gained since about 1968 (or if you're 20, all the weight you'll gain in the next twenty years).

First Step—Trimming Fat Nouns

As a first step in moving from a more static to a more dynamic style, you can "lighten" heavy nouns by using "thinner" nouns. You can spot these heavy nouns with their endings that make them even heavier, like "-ation" or "-ability" or "-ment."

Consider Replacing These Heavy Nouns	With These Lighter Nouns.
application, utilization	use
compensation, remuneration	pay, salary
conceptualization	idea, draft, plan
condition, situation	state, status
determination	choice
finalization	end
implementation	start, use
indication	sign
location	site, place
prioritization	ranking, rank
reservation	doubt
capability	ability
capable	able
irascible	grumpy, angry
irreconcilable	stubborn
irrefutability	true
methodology	method, way
noticeable	clear

| plethora | many |
| requirement | need |

You may spot a few real favorites (and indicators) here of people who feel so insecure about their ideas that they feel they need to resort to linguistic signs to impress others. Besides avoiding such indicators yourself, you can watch for unnecessarily verbose language[30] as a tip off to spot weak ideas that speakers and/or writers have sought to fortify verbally.

© alex74/Shutterstock.com

"I'm disinclined to acquiesce to your request. Means 'no'."

---

[30] Poser words.

SECOND STEP—MOVING FROM NOUNS TO VERBS

Yes, you can trim the fat off some heavy nouns. Better yet, you can actually transform overweight nouns into dynamic and moving verbs. Showing action, verbs usually communicate doing something. Verbs include words like "play," "run," "move," "do," "accomplish," "motivate." Your language will become more clear, graceful, and powerful when you replace big, fat nouns with words that <u>move</u>.

Consider Replacing These Heavy Nouns →	**With These Verbs.**
application →	apply

I wrote an **application** for a managerial position.
   vs. I **applied** for a managerial position.

capability →	can

The latest I-phone has the **capability** of photographing ghosts.
   Vs. The latest I-phone **can** photograph ghosts.

compensation →	compensate

So, how do you plan to get **compensation** for the extra workers?
  vs. So, how do you plan to **compensate** the extra workers?
  still better: So, how do you plan to **pay** the extra workers?

conceptualization →	conceptualize

She came up with a great **conceptualization** for a marketing strategy.
  vs. She **conceptualized** a great marketing strategy.
  Still better: She **drafted** a great marketing strategy.

EXERCISE

Now it's your turn. Improve the "heavy" sentences by replacing the nouns with verbs:

| **Replace These Heavy Nouns** | → | **With These Verbs.** |

---

dependence → depend

Some lawyers have a **dependence** on wordiness.

Some lawyers _____ on wordiness.

---

determination → determine

Management should make an on-site **determination** regarding wind damage.

Management should _____ on-site wind damage.

---

finalization → finalize

Please create a **finalization** of the plan.

Please _____ the plan.

---

implementation → implement

We will begin the **implementation** of the new policy March 15.

We will _____ the new policy March 15.

---

indication → indicate

Clients should give some **indication** when they feel dissatisfied.

Clients should _____.

_____

interaction → interact

I'd like to see more effective **interaction** at your facility.

I'd like you _____.

_____

requirements → require

What are your client's **requirements** for the project?

What _____?

_____

reservation → reserve

He made a **reservation** for a table of eight for 6:00 tomorrow evening.

He _____.

_____

authorization → _____

Has he given his **authorization** on the paperwork yet?

Has he _____?

_____

Now, clarify these sentences by changing the big heavy nouns to verbs.

How high was your water utilization this month?
_____?

The ambulance will not provide transportation for more than three patients at a time.
_____.

Please submit a statement for funds needed for facilitation of the plan.
_____.

I need a statement outlining the costs for maintenance of one patient for one year.
_____.

What are the fees for entrance into the academy?
_____?

Presented with chocolate, I have a tendency to indulge.
_____.

Using heavy nouns can bring complications to legal proceedings.
_____.

You have given yourself quite enough brain stimulation for one evening.
_____.

STYLE PRINCIPLE NUMBER FIVE

Take the little words out.

Little words often work their way into spoken and written discourse in subconscious, sneaky ways and sit right smack dab in the best places to put informative, interesting language. Insidious little creatures. Now that you have learned to avoid adding big words just for their own sake, you can learn to take the little words out. As you take the cluttering little words out, the words that actually communicate something will stand out more.

The little words ripping you off of good places to put your brilliant ideas come primarily as two kinds: pronouns and verbs of being. Together they form really stupid sentences like, "it is," "they are," "this was," that communicate just about nothing. Our language also has little meaningless phrases that we stick in when our brains have nothing more meaningful to add. Teachers call this "filler"; they can spot this filler a mile away and feel insulted that student writers think teachers have nothing better to do than read it.

Random Filler. Here are some examples of random filler to edit out of your writing. Perhaps you secretly know of all sorts of other favorite filler you can eliminate from your writing also.

"in today's society" — Dump and take a look at the subject of your sentence. If your sentence subject is really generic (like "people"), replace it with something specific that informs your reader what you are talking about. For example, you could change "In today's society people just don't care about garbage" to "White-collar, beer-guzzling, week-end warriors just don't care about garbage in our local park." Get the picture?

(of the principle here – not the trashed park!)

"there are" — Dump it and make whatever you are talking about the subject of your sentence. For example, you could change "There are a whole bunch of leaves on the lawn" to "A whole bunch of leaves fell on the lawn." "A whole bunch of leaves has piled up on the lawn." Or, you could change, "There are several explanations for the results of this experiment" to "The results of this experiment suggest several explanations." Notice that when you dump "there are" or "there is," you can usually replace the "are" or "is" with some spiffy (informative, interesting) verb.

"people" — Just say who you are talking about. The more specific you can be, the greater your credibility. For example, you can change, "People should not leave smelly running clothes lying all over the bathroom floor" to "Considerate room-mates should not leave smelly running clothes lying all over the bathroom floor." Or you could change "People in ancient Greece enjoyed the Olympics" to "Adult Athenian male citizens enjoyed the Greek Olympics."

"nowadays" — Again, just say when and where you are trying to situate your ideas. For example, you can change "People don't like to pay taxes nowadays" to "Disillusioned post-Vietnam US citizens don't like to pay current taxes."

"whatever" — You can translate this into the Latin "etc.," the abbreviation for "and other stuff," but in academic writing you're better off just omitting such slang. If your concept really does call for slang, be sure to put it in quotation marks.[31] You can get away with just about anything you put in quotation marks.

---

[31] Native American student, Jessica Brittenham calls these "bunny ears."

If you get that sick sort of feeling that you need to add words just to make your essay longer, resist. Go back to the first element of Cicero's rhetorical canon, invention (Chapter 3, Invention), and reconsider what sort of information you have for your essay. Add information, not just mushy words. If you have lots of introspective narrative, add some details or cold wisdom from the library. If you have lots of library stuff, add some of your own ideas/perceptions. And so on.

Pronouns. Pronouns sure do take the place of a noun. They often take the place of all sorts of other good materials too. They look like ~~this~~ the following: this, that, it, he, she, him, her, they, these. Replace the pesky little usurpers of meaning with some more interesting or informative language. You don't have to replace *all* pronouns, but do replace those where you could add information. While you're at it, you can also replace generalized words like "people" or "thing."
For example:

> Susan Warner wrote *The Wide, Wide World* in 1850. In it, she shows readers how they might struggle to become better people.

To edit, you scan through your draft and circle the pronouns (and other annoyances) with a fat purple crayon:

> Susan Warner wrote *The Wide, Wide World* in 1850. In (it,) (she) shows readers how (they) might struggle to become better (people.)

Then take the little words out, replacing with some information:

> Susan Warner wrote *The Wide, Wide World* in 1850. In ~~it~~ what would become America's first million-selling novel, ~~she~~ the much imitated author shows readers how ~~they~~ anyone intent on living a more full life might struggle to become ~~better people~~ a more selfless and forthright person.

Naturally, you need to have information in order to replace pronouns. The beauty to replacing pronouns with information is that you will have to start looking around and investigating your world a bit more. Replacing pronouns forces you to become more inquisitive and perceptive. Instead of just saying, "Gee, it's[32] a nice day," you get into the habit of contemplating what you are saying. You try to determine the criteria for (in this case) "a nice day." Then you put all that criteria where the "it" used to go: "Gee, this cold north wind combining with lots of moisture-laden air coming in from the coast promises a nice powder snow day up on the mountain."

Savvy?

Replacing pronouns has one more advantage; doing so provides a secret solution for the gender mess that our language is now wallowing through. This principle of style goes, "When in doubt, bail out." Back in the old days of Miss and Mrs., singular nouns took singular pronouns and the people-nouns all took he or him—unless the sentence could add some good solid sexism, like doctors ➔ he/him; nurses ➔ she/her; teachers ➔ she/her; principals & professors ➔ he/him; secretary ➔ she/her; boss ➔ he/him.[33] Your author learned that "correct" English for non-gender specific people nouns went, "Everyone should return his library books" and "A good doctor/lawyer/entrepreneur takes his education seriously." So after a zillion years of this sort of language conditioning, some uppity women did not want to use language conventions to condition their daughters into gender roles any more. Language changed. Some self-proclaimed authorities invented the new word, "s/he"; this form is now outdated—perhaps because the him or her combo might become "hi/r" or "he/m"? Then for a while some well meaning women just started to

---

[32] "It's" equals "it is." "Its" means something belongs to "it."
[33] Gee, maybe the statistic that US working women earn $77 for every $100 that men earn has something to do with linguistic conditioning.

use "she" and "her" for all people nouns, perhaps embarking on a corrective crusade of reverse sexism. Then (my favorite) the practice of switching back and forth between "he" and "she" became popular: "The student picked up her backpack and straightening his shirt walked to her next class where he sat down in her favorite desk anticipating his sweetie to walk in any minute." Finally, some writers still use the "he/she" and "her/him" forms. Most language buffs consider these forms out-dated edging up on wrong probably because of the "him/herself" mess. Currently, you're safe to write out all the words as real words: "he or she"; "him or her"; "him- or herself."[34] The best solution for all this, however, is to bail out. Don't do any of this stuff. Just cheat and make your nouns plural so that you can use "their." Plural nouns also add information.

Yucky: Everyone should pick up his or her towels.
Better: Slobs should pick up their towels.

Yucky: Everyone should think for him- or herself.
Better: Students reading this book should think for themselves.

Yucky: A person should take care of his or her shoes.
Better: People should take care of their shoes.
Even better: Back-packers should take care of their shoes.

---

[34] Do not fall into the really annoying misuse of "myself" for not knowing when to use "me." Use "myself" only when you've already said your name (or "I") in the same sentence. Bad: Give the form to Ms. Smith or myself. Good: Give the form to Ms. Smith or me. Good: I chuckled to myself.

Ah ha! Check it out. Here language moves from generic old pronouns and might-as-well-be-pronoun words like "people" to more specific nouns and noun phrases. That is, by bailing out of this whole gender pronoun mess, you can replace awkwardness with more informative language. And vice-versa, by using more communicative words (especially in the plural), you can avoid the whole volatile "he or she" business.

Exercise

Commercial media such as television seeks to please and fascinate the greatest possible number of viewers. The median vocabulary and syntax that Americans can now handle has now reached about the eighth-grade level. To attract more readers (consumers) some newspapers are now using a fourth grade vocabulary. Chronic television patrons get a steady dose of eighth-grade level vocabulary and syntax—perpetuating that language level and making television an excellent source of pronouns. Choose a couple of pronoun-packed sentences from the media (internet, billboards, TV, newspapers, etc.) and practice replacing as many pronouns as you can with some information. (It's OK to have fun and make them goofy.)

Verbs of Being. Verbs of being show that something exists. Since most things exist (in order to be things), saying that those things exist becomes silly and boring. Verbs of being add boredom to your writing. These little stealers include such words as "be, are, is, were, was." Current academic style prefers jazzier verbs. This principle of language fashion takes off from the historical explanation earlier in this chapter. A few decades ago when our culture and language appreciated big heavy things, people got very accustomed to using verbs of being. Maybe things were so heavy that they just sat there; that is, maybe things just "were." So 50's people said things like,

"That book is interesting."

"This class is boring."

"My grade was an "A.""

Notice how all these tips for upgrading your style begin to fit together. You can add agents as subjects of sentences, dump the verbs of being, and use spiffier, more informative verbs all at once. Just meander down the sentence and find some word to change into a nifty verb. If you can't find one, stick some person into your sentence and show that person actively *doing* something.

That book interests me. / I found the book interesting.

I enjoyed the interesting book.

This class bores me. / In this stale class a cadaverous professor reviews vapid eighth-grade material in a monotone of F flat.

My grade was an "A." / I earned an "A."

You need either a word processor (click "edit," then "find," then do a search for "is, are") or else a handful of nickels, a fat purple crayon, and a five-year old. Give the kid a nickel for every "is," "was," "are," "were," that the little money-hungry critter can circle. Then, instead of saying that something just "is," show something going on or someone doing something.

And on the subject of verbs, academic style now prefers the "correct" use of voice: passive, active, and conditional, which brings us to the question →

Where Were You When Life Was Lived?

"Smith, party of four, can *be seated*."

"Passengers of flight 486 can *be met* at Gate A-16."

"All seatbelts should now *be fastened*."

"Four books will *be read* in American Lit., 255."

Do you sometimes feel you're having an out-of-body life experience watching activity around you "be done"? How can you "be seated" unless you sit down? How can those passengers "be met" unless someone meets them? How do the seatbelts "be fastened" without someone to fasten them? And those fat books in English 255—"be read"—sure, I imagine they'll *be read* by someone or another, but who says *I* need to read them?

Consider your stance toward life. You may well consider yourself active, functional, able, and willing to act, react, transact, do, and exert energy in your own or others' behalf. Few people wish a life spent passively as a Kafkaesque[35] cog in the corporate machine. Rather, we fancy grabbing life by the vitals and taking the road less traveled.[36]

© eirimis/Shutterstock.com

---

[35] Huh?? To get depressed regarding being passive, read some Kafka ~~
[36] Thank you, Robert Frost

From *Walden: Or, Life in the Woods*
"I went to the woods because I wished to live deliberately, to front only the essential facts of life, and see if I could not learn what it had to teach, and not, when I came to die, discover that I had not lived. I did not wish to live what was not life, living is so dear; nor did I wish to practice resignation, unless it was quite necessary. I wanted to live deep and suck out all the marrow of life . . ."

— Henry David Thoreau, 1854

Interestingly, our cultural language throws up some real mental roadblocks, often thwarting our abilities to exert autonomy. Fortunately, you can learn to recognize these linguistic roadblocks and, with some simple equipment, learn to turn them to your advantage. One big trick here lies in getting to know the active and passive voices. Active voice has to do with somebody doing something. (Leon read the book. Leon actively did something.) Passive voice has to do with somebody (or thing) having something done to it. (The book was read. The book was passive to someone doing something to it.)

WHAT IS GOING ON:

Properly used, the passive voice communicates that someone or something was passive or perhaps even a victim to some action: Gertie was raped; Fred was beat up; English teachers are underpaid. Conceptualizing some objects as passive to activity, however, sometimes gets a little strange. Why, for example, should a book be considered passive to being read? Was it ripped, scribbled in, dog-eared and left out in the rain? Why should a seatbelt be considered being passive to being fastened? Was it somehow violated by some pervert fascinated with its action? Worse, when we consider events around us happening passively, we rob ourselves from the sense that we can function actively—read books, fasten belts, meet people, and sit down to dinner. Events around us keep happening while we feel removed and diminished by our own inactivity. So how can we begin to deal with the passivity and activity in the language that daily bombards us and that culture fixes in our heads? Simple: By identifying the passive voice in what we hear and read, we can recognize as phantom-rhetorical a would-be power that renders us ineffectual. Also, by identifying the passive voice in our own utterances, we can use it correctly to enhance rather than confuse communication.

To spot passive voice, look for a combination of two or maybe three elements:

1. A verb of being, those little words such as "be, is, was, were, am, have, are, etc." Also look for words like "felt" or "seemed."
2. A word that ends in -en, -t, -nt, -d, -ed.[37] Examples: beaten, sought, sent, told, smashed, trounced, clobbered, denied, fried, tried, jilted, tilted, and left.
3. (Sometimes) the who-dun-it give-away word, "by."

Put these three together and you have a rhythm like, "the lights were dimmed, the cards were dealt, four shots were poured, three shots were heard, and a heavy thudding was noticed.

AN UNDERCOVER AGENT

The danger of the passive voice comes when a speaker or writer uses it to hide the identity of who did the deed that the subject passively endures: "Community workers may have their salaries cut." By using passive construction, this writer cleverly hides who or what agency might actively cut salaries. Asking "by whom" when you hear the passive voice makes people bring the agent out of hiding: "Community workers may have their salaries cut by a voter initiative financed by wealthy investors." Turn that construction to the active voice to focus on the agent: "Wealthy investors started an initiative to cut community workers' salaries." If your brother-in-law, Tony, has been out robbing banks again, you can hide your knowledge of his involvement in his latest heist with the handy passive: "Citizens' Bank was robbed again today." Here you communicate that the bank was a passive victim of some action. Using the active voice, discloses Tony, "Tony robbed the Citizens' Bank today." Notice that you can tell something of a speaker/writer's stance by his or her use of active or passive voice.

---

[37] These are called "past participles," if anyone *is* interest*ed*. (Joke – get it?—Are you passive to your own interest? Hummmmm?)

Does the speaker want you to focus on the person passive to some action (Aunt Tilly was run over by a Mack truck)? Does the speaker want you to focus on the person who actively did something (Some jerk in a Mack Truck ran over Aunt Tilly)? Or is the speaker trying to hide something from you (Aunt Tilly was run over)?

Speakers seeking to hide behind the force of large institutions (e.g., government, military, academia) seem to find a voice of authority in the passive voice. By reporting that "troops were sent," "money was spent," "decisions were reached," institutions can focus reader/listener attention on the action while protecting the identities of those who sent the troops, spent the moneys, or reached decisions. Also, the voice of authority often puts "you" into a situation where "you" cannot act; you are condemned to passivity in the face of semantic authority. "Trespassers will be prosecuted." "Students with overdue books will be denied course credit." "Employees will be subject to drug testing." Once again, the speaker hides the identity of the person/s who actively prosecute, deny credit, and subject others to testing. Further, the recipient of these messages, denied the information of whomever renders them powerless, becomes "subject to" the action of some mystical, powerful, unknown Force. Pretty scary.

Note: occasionally, in the struggle to recognize passive voice, students confuse "passive voice" with "past tense." These terms both start with "pa." That's about all they have in common. Past tense has to do with time—concepts like yesterday or long ago, like the *past*. That elusive natural resource, time, has very little to do with who is actively doing something and who is passively getting the brunt of something done. In academic style just use tenses to note time—simple, except for one little bit of craziness.[38] Use the present tense to discuss what anyone says in a reference—even if that person said that something long ago in the past and is dead. This craziness means that you will sometimes have two tenses—two time things—going on in the same sentence—very bizarre. For example: Poor old dead Abraham Lincoln wrote the Gettysburg Address a long time ago (note that "wrote" is past tense); in it he says, "blah, blah, blah" (note that "says" is present tense). Use the present tense whenever a book "says" something (and try to use a less boring verb than "says"). Evidently, words never die. Back to active and passive voice ~~

Active Voice	**Passive Voice**
Last summer I *baby-sat* my kid's pet pig, Bacon. My son *brought* Bacon in as a cute little piglet and Bacon gradually *transformed* into a self-centered spoiled pet porker.	Last summer I *was blessed* with taking care of my kid's pet pig, Bacon. Bacon *was brought* in as a cute little piglet and gradually *was transformed* into a self-centered spoiled pet porker.

See the difference? In the active voice, people and pig *do* things. In the passive voice, not only do person and pig have something done to them, but also the reader never learns who should take responsibility for the pet pig—a hidden agent.

---

[38] Never try to "make sense" of grammar and/or language customs. Humans have all gotten together to create language and so have created a great deal of cultural weirdness. What's even weirder is when would-be grammarians try to judge people or ideas by the alleged "right" or "wrong" of grammar. Real grammarians use grammar as a tool to figure out the agenda lying beneath the mere meaning of the words themselves—as you are learning to do now with a heightened awareness of voice.

What to Do with Passive Voice: Incoming

If you recognize this pattern in language you hear or read, determine why the speaker or writer uses it: to hide an agent from you; to foist some institutional voice of authority on you; or (more honestly) to show someone or thing as actually passive to some action. If you discern an incoming passive meant to trip you up, diffuse it—ask for the agent "yeah, by whom?" or "yeah, sez who?" Rhetorical nastiness constitutes a party foul and gives "rhetoric" a bad name. If you come across a passive starting with an "it" and ending with a "that," run away. Cancel marriages, quit jobs, fire employees, drop classes, remove from your life any time you hear or read, "it was recommended that," "it can be seen that," "it was shown that," "it was specified that," "it was directed that," "it was decided that." Here, the speaker puts his or her message in a subordinate, secondary clause not as important as telling you that some nebulous, undefined, imaginary "it" just got passive to being specified, directed, decided. The phrase tells you that like the "it," you, too, must stand idly by and believe the message because you believe in magic rhetorical power. Just say "no." Translate immediately to: "someone here consciously or unconsciously is laying an insidious aggressive trip on me and I figured it out." Then given your insight, deal with the situation. This construction works great out of the mouth of Dr. Strangelove, but spells doomsday to communication.

What to Do with Passive Voice: Outgoing

If you recognize in your own thoughts, utterances, writing, a situation where something is being passive to an action that just doesn't make sense, fix it. Figure out who is doing something and say so. Often, trying to come up with a subject provides you with new insight. "My favorite vitamins were taken off the shelf and made available only through prescription." Where's the subject? Ask yourself "who dun it"? The shopkeeper? Naaah. The F.D.A.? Maybe. Pharmaceutical Companies who want me to pay prescription prices for my favorite vitamins? You're getting closer. Moving from the passive to active voice in your own thinking forces you to look into situations that you can easily ignore by using the passive voice. Create a sentence that communicates more specific information: "Lobbyists for Acme Drugs convinced the F.D.A. to take my favorite vitamins off the shelf and make them available only through prescription."

If you find yourself uttering refrains such as, "it has been found that," dump the whole atrocity and gain some confidence in what you are communicating. Move from "it has been found that Dad's apple pie tastes better than Mom's" to the more confident, "Dad's apple pie tastes better than Mom's." Hedging to spare someone else's feelings often results in diminishing your own sense of self. If Mom's around, say something else.

By gaining an awareness of the passive and active voices, you can grow from using them in an often harmful habitual manner to using them to effect honest and meaningful communication. By all means, do use the passive voice when you wish to show your subject passive to an action: "the river is dreadfully polluted." And use the active voice when you wish to show who actively does something: "Clear-cutting dreadfully pollutes the river." Using the passive and active voices intentionally will relieve you of the appearing full of hot air and relying on an institution voice rather than your own. Intentional usage will also nudge you toward self-honesty, enhanced confidence in your own thoughts, and more clear and healthy communication with others.

SOME PRACTICE WITH ACTIVE AND PASSIVE VOICE

You can communicate what you mean to communicate more clearly when you control your use of active and passive voice. There's nothing worse than trying to urge people to <u>act</u> using <u>passive</u> voice.[39] First step: Figure out when you want to show activity and when you want to show passivity.

Good passive: "Fred was beat up." "After six hours of labor, Gertie was exhausted." "I was snowed in." These sentences show that the subjects (Fred, Gertie, and I) were all passive to outside forces. And so the passive voice very nicely shows what the writer wants to show.

Bad passive: "This exercise will be finished by tomorrow." "Your power will be cut off." "Mistakes were made." These sentences all pretty much hide, protect, or excuse the subject. To have respect and/or tell the truth, the writer can add a "who dun it" agent or person.

- "This exercise will *be finished* by tomorrow." **Who** is going to finish the exercise? The writer should have some respect for students and so put students into the sentence: "Students will finish this exercise by tomorrow."

- "The power of those with delinquent accounts will *be cut* off." **Who** will cut off the power? "The Henry County Power Authority will cut off the power of those with delinquent accounts."

- "Mistakes *were made*." **Who** made the mistakes? "In his 1987 State of the Union address Reagan famously hid making mistakes by using the passive voice to say 'mistakes were made.'"

---

[39] "Protestors wishing to protest X should *be gathered* (passive voice) at the park at 10:00." Arrrrgggghhhh. Try "Protestors wishing to protest X, please gather at the park at 10:00."

Your turn. Are these sentences better voiced in active voice or in passive voice? Why?

"Grandma was run over by a reindeer." (You care more about Grandma than the reindeer.)
☐ Leave as is. Why?   ☐ Change. Why?

_____
_____
_____

"I was grounded." (You want to express that you were victimized.)
☐ Leave as is. Why?   ☐ Change. Why?

_____
_____
_____

"The bank was robbed." (You have no clue who robbed the bank and you rather like the bank.)
☐ Leave as is. Why?   ☐ Change. Why?

_____
_____
_____

"The bank was robbed." (You were one of the four western bad guys who robbed the bank and you want to remain unknown.)

☐ Leave as is. Why?   ☐ Change. Why?

_____
_____
_____

_____

"The bank was robbed." (You were one of the four western bad guys who robbed the bank and the sheriff just offered you a deal that you go free if you rat on your three partners.)

☐ Leave as is. Why?   ☐ Change. Why?

_____
_____
_____

_____

Now some less philosophical editing. Change these passive voice sentences to active voice **by adding a human or some agent**.

"The cookies were stolen from the cookie jar." Add an agent: Fred? The monkey? My imaginary friend?

_____
_____
_____

_____

"While driving home, I was pulled over last night." Add an agent: The California State Highway Patrol? The broken tie rod in my steering system? A very nice police officer?

_____
_____
_____.

Change the passive to active by making the "by _____" the agent. Then sort of read the sentence backwards.

"Lily's meticulously kept lawn was trashed <u>by gophers</u>."

<u>   Gophers trashed   </u>
<u>   </u>.

Sam's grade point average was brought down a notch by that last exam.

_____
_____.

The refrigerator was messed up by Granny's exploding homemade rootbeer.

_____
_____.

Sally's flourishing garden was pretty much destroyed by deer last night.

_____
_____.

My patience was greatly stressed by having to switch a bunch of passive voice sentences to active voice sentences.

_____
_____.

Now you can control active and passive voice in your own writing!

More Language Awareness: The Conditional
Woulda, Shoulda, Coulda, But...

Flowing through volcanic high desert bluffs, the Deschutes River provides anglers and kayakers with alternating stretches of exhilarating white-water and pastoral beauty. Kayaking and basking in a particularly lovely stretch, my otherwise overworked urban companion remarks, "Yes, I could really get to enjoy this."

"Could," if what? Go on and enjoy! Sometimes our language holds us in jail, robbing us from experiencing what we don't even realize we're missing. Some of these iron bars appear in the form of internalized, assumed, insidious, and habitual "conditions." Conditions of what? Big Brother? Super-ego? Old age? Darth Vader?

Consider: "When I was a kid, I'd climb trees."
Here, "I'd" hides "I would." I *would* climb trees if what? If I ate all my vegetables? If I did all my homework? If I didn't get caught in Farmer Fred's orchard? Some condition lurks in the "would" and prevents the would-be tree-climber from having a clear, clean, flat-out good memory. Or another, "I remember Sally; she'd ride through the meadow, her skirts and red hair an extension of Dobbin's flying mane." Again, the "'d" covers up a "she would," and the remembered scene lingers somewhere as a semi-illusion. The task here involves bringing that illusion into an actual part of one's past: bringing "Sally would ride" to "Sally rode." By reestablishing (correcting) the memory, we can begin to reestablish the nature of the self. Tackle your conditional past in thought, conversation, and writing, and see who you become.

While you come to grips with the past, you also need to face the here and now. Do you put your present aside, locked in some linguistic habit that renders you alienated from pushing the save-button, the whoopee-button, the holy-cow-check-this-out-button? The task here involves moving the kayaker's "I could really enjoy" the simple, "I am enjoying," or "I enjoy!" What's the obstacle here: a fear of lawsuits, the Puritan ethic, "Shame on you, you're having too much fun!"? Fixing our linguistic orientation to our capacity to act enables us to unleash real possibilities. Naturally, we can't eliminate the conditional completely. (Or can we?) "Gee, I'd love to dump this job and embark on a quest for the perfect taco." But job or no job, we can still come face to face with our desires: move the "I would love to" closer toward honestly facing "I want to." Getting beyond the "would, should, ought," gets us closer to exploring just what the conditions of the conditional voice entail. "I'd love to dump this job," (but I've got family to support) may depict possibilities different from "I'd love to dump this job," (but I wouldn't know what to do with myself). Recognizing the conditional "I would" and moving to "I want to dump this job, but I do not know what to do with myself" can lead to "Gee, I'll explore some possibilities."

Armed with remembered memories and new possibilities for the present, you (should? might? ought to? had best?) consider the future. Consider the graphic engineer: "of course, I'd be able to get the report in on Thursday." Both to speaker and to listener, "I'd" neatly covers the "I would" admission that this engineer will encounter or subconsciously try to create some situation or other to miss the deadline. "I would be able to get the report in"—right, "*would*" if what? If you don't go skiing? If the dog doesn't eat your laptop? If you really intended to? If you had a bonus dangling in front of your nose? Business people prefer success to failure, so they often make statements that herald success and protect them from appearing prone to playing the loser. The conditional has its place and function; use "would, should, or could" to yourself and others when you consciously acknowledge some condition keeping you from doing something. That is, get rid of the conditional for the easy tasks, and clearly state the conditions for the tasks you feel unsure about. Use language to communicate clearly your view of your capabilities and the future: "I can get the report in on Thursday" or "I can get the report in on Thursday if . . . ." then name your conditions.

> ### PSYCHOLINGUISTIC SELF-DEFENSE
>
> Cinderella: Gee, I would really love to go to the ball (but . . .).
> Fairy Godmother: Whoa – the conditions involved here are really going to take some work: carriage, dress, bath, instant education, total make-over.
>
>
>
> Haggard Student trying to buy some coffee: One mocha, double shot, grandee, please.
> Barista: That would be $4.45.
> Haggard Student: Would be if what – If I had sprinkles? I don't want 'em.
> Barista: Right. No sprinkles. That would be $4.45.
> Haggard Student: Would be if what – if it came in a cup?
> Barista: Right. It comes in a cup. That would be $4.45.
> Haggard Student: Would be if WHAT ?!?!?!
>
>
>
> Loser Guy trying to pick up on a woman in a tavern: Gee, I'd really like to take you out sometime. I'm free next Friday. How 'bout it?
> Grammatically astute Woman: Hummm. "I'd really like to . . . ." (A) The subject of this guy's sentence is "I." – What an egotistical jerk.
> (B) "would like to" – if/but what? He had a job? He didn't have a wife and five kids? I weren't so ugly? 👎 Forget it, thanks.
> Grammatically astute Guy tries: Gee, would you like to have dinner next Friday?
> Grammatically astute Woman: [Hummm. "Would you . . . ?" (A) He puts ME in the subject place – considers me a functional decision-making human being – how sweet! (B) He offers me the room to decline gracefully by offering that "would" to me – I could make up, "gee, would love to but . . . with a string of conditions." What a nice guy!]   👍 Sure, sounds lovely.

ONE MORE VOICE: THE IMPERATIVE

With the imperative voice a speaker literally orders people around. Its secret is the invisible and understood subject, "you." Examples of the imperative voice:

- "Take out the trash" is the same as "You take out the trash."
- "Stop" is the same as the full sentence (because it has both a subject and a verb), "You stop."
- "You work with me here" is the same as the imperative voice, "Work with me here."

Got the idea? (You got the idea?)[40]

Of note regarding imperative voice – You've probably heard your academic writing instructors tell you to avoid using "you" in your college essays and papers. Good idea. Don't use "you" because (A) doing so makes assumptions about your reader and can be construed as impolite and (B) you shouldn't need to resort of such rhetorical ploys to draw your reader in. Your ideas should be sufficiently strong to engage your readers. That is, in academic writing your brilliant ideas should be so clearly put that you need no bells and whistles to reinforce their impact on readers. By virtue of their solid, graceful, uncluttered presentation, your good ideas should be able to stand on their own.

Just as you should not have to resort to using "you" in academic writing, you should not have to resort to using the imperative voice because the imperative voice has that hidden and assumed "you" right there as the invisible subject of your sentence. Using the imperative voice in academic writing comes across to your professors or other academic readers as impolite. Do not find yourself ordering your professors around—very uncool. Avoid writing things like "Imagine flying . . . ." or "Consider the idea that . . ."

---

[40] Can a question be "imperative"? Your author has no clue.

And for your own psycholinguistic sanity, be alert to incoming imperative voice. Notice the bossy imperative quality of politicians' speeches that order, "Make no mistake . . . ." or "Let me repeat . . . ." or "Let me be clear . . . ." Beware of all the voices, lurking in the language that comes to you and that you use!⁴¹

The route to linguistic health (not lying to yourself) and functional communication (healthy interpersonal relationships) involves becoming aware of our own culturally learned tendencies to limit thoughts and actions to some conditions that we can't even fathom. Language can remove human beings from their own subjectivity. Language can encourage our passivity. Voices in language can subject us to unexplained conditions and can order us around. But you can now recognize all these voices. Language need not unconsciously restrict our thoughts and actions. Properly used, we can actually make language generate new life possibilities. The prescription? Ah ha—just pinch yourself at every "would," "should," and "ought to."⁴² Once you become aware of your own linguistic habits—those that separate you from your past, prevent you from acknowledging present activities, and squelch your possibilities for the future—you can begin to act on that awareness. You, too, can enjoy the river.

Some Extra Reading

Here are some pointers from others who have a bit to say about current style. Californian, Dr. Paul Roberts ("How to Say Nothing in Five Hundred Words") taught English and linguistics and wrote several English texts, popular in the 1950s and 1960s. George Orwell ["Politics and the English Language" (1946)] is probably best

---

⁴¹ You got it – In even this sentence lurks the imperative voice—telling you to beware.
⁴² And conditional cousins, the modals—may and might—and such other hedgers as perhaps, kind of, sort of, someday, maybe, ya know.

known for his novels that argue against totalitarianism: *Animal Farm* (1945) and *1984* (1949). Kurt Vonnegut ["How to Write with Style" (1981)] has written several novels that make great summer reading. And if you are really interested, write to the Office of Investor Education and Assistance, U.S. Securities and Exchange Commission, 450 5th Street, N.W., Washington D.C. 20549 for a copy of *the Plain English Handbook—How to Create Clear SEC Disclosure Documents*. This document of how to write documents more or less repeats what you have learned about style from this chapter. So with what you now know of writing, you're set to hit Washington.

© lynea/Shutterstock.com

VI
Memory
Or
Keeping your Head Together

"Memory is the firm mental grasp of matter and words."
—Cicero. *de Inventione*.

"Memory—what a strange thing it is!—does not record concrete duration . . . .
We are unable to relive duration that has been destroyed. We can only think of it,
in the line of an abstract time that is deprived of all thickness.
—Gaston Bachelard. *The Poetics of Space*.

"If you remember the '60's, you weren't there."
—Traditional Saying

Current composition theorists and writing teachers pretty much skip over the fourth element of the Cicero's method, memory. Compared to the volumes of advice regarding the other elements of rhetoric—invention, arrangement, style, and delivery—even Cicero practically dismisses memory saying, "In my opinion, a strong memory is a gift of nature and not something gained from rule books" (*De Oratore*. II 350). Before approaching the ancient "gift vs. learned" controversy regarding memory, you might like to consider more current views.

At first glance, except for a few traditionally-minded school teachers, our culture seems to neglect learning the powers of memory. Customarily, we engage more in passive than in active memory. Resigned to put into our memories what the culture would have there, we fill our minds more with quantifiers than with qualitative material. Most of the quantifiers that our culture has given us to put into our minds act to position or locate us.[1] A typical American memory might store various birthdays, a social security number, a few "personal identification numbers" (PINs), and the numerical street address on a numbered street in a city located by zip code. A memory might hold several phone numbers: one's own and that of childhood. As a typical driver, I know the year and model of my car and almost remember the license plate number. I remember my neighbor's license plate number because my neighbor was not passive to a quantifier, but chose a qualitative material for his plate: a word.

Also in my memory are all the lyrics of the music that happened to be popular at various times in my life: Stones, Cream, Country Joe, Janis, Jimi, and traditional jazz standards. I did not consciously put all these lyrics into my memory; they ended up there by virtue of my sliding into time and place where/when their repetition made them stick. The more qualitative the stuff in my memory, the more consciously I have had to stick it there: favorite ideas, quotations, poetry, etc. But generally, like most folks, I have been passive and neglectful of exercising my memory.

> "The discovery of the alphabet will create forgetfulness in the learners' souls, because they will not use their memories." — Plato: *The Phaedrus* and quoted by Marshall McLuhan in *The Medium is the Massage* (113).

---

[1] "The more the data banks record about each one of us, the less we exist." —Marshall McLuhan (from *Playboy*, 1969). **That was in 1969!!!!!**

A Fable

Having gone away for years and returning to my home town on the craggy Pacific coastline, I found myself one evening in a small, close redwood tavern—the kind where everyone knows everyone else, historically if not personally. Returning the academician, allegedly smart in things literate, I took the stool center, which would shortly become a hot seat. I had not expected a confrontation. The tavern-keep had arms that flashed deftly from bottles to glasses to napkins, seemingly quite independent from his steady eyes, firm amid the wild array of dancing hair and scarves. His tasks at last momentarily settled, and whirling around in slow motion with only the length of the bar to cage him in, he spoke. We had stumbled upon the power of the performance poet. And we were the ones caught.

I learned that evening the weakness of secondary sources. I learned the fluff of analysis in the face of memory. I learned that memory—so easily overlooked and forgotten—may well be the most pivotal element of the Ciceronian canon: the very crux that makes or breaks things literate. I learned from the attack of the mad barkeep poet that memory determines the nature of discourse, elevating our experience of and relationship to the word from that of mere spectators to players in a participation sport. It is memory that transforms us from spectators to participants around the campfire or (with lines and lyrics ready) at the *Rocky Horror Picture Show*, *The Search for the Holy Grail*, or following the lyrical shows of one's favorite rock group, or with sing-alongs.

As such, memory takes us from our lonely individual lives of quiet desperation to a participatory experience in the cultural community of the word. Memory offers us a sort of tribalness: folk songs, childhood stories, traditional recipes. Perhaps we enjoy so little of this tribal joy here early in the twenty-first century because of writing. Near the end of *Phaedrus* Plato warns how writing threatens memory:

MYTH OF THE INVENTION OF WRITING

[Socrates tells the story of the Egyptian god, Theuth, who invented number and calculation, geometry and astronomy and above all writing. Presenting his arts to the Egyptian king, Thamus, Theuth said of writing,] "Here, O king, is a branch of learning that will make the people of Egypt wiser and improve their memories: my discovery [writing] provides a recipe for memory and wisdom." But the king answered and said "O man full of arts, to one it is given to create the things of art, and to another to judge what measure of harm and of profit they have for those who will use them. And so it is that you, by reason of your tender regard for the writing that is your offspring, have declared the very opposite of its true effect. If men learn this, it will implant forgetfulness in their souls: they will cease to exercise memory because they rely on that which is written, calling things to remembrance no longer from within themselves, but by means of external marks; what you have discovered is a recipe not for memory, but for reminder. And it is no true wisdom that you offer your disciples, but only its semblance; for by telling them of many things without teaching them, you will make them seem to know much, while for the most part they know nothing; and as men filled, not with wisdom, but with the conceit of wisdom, they will be a burden to their fellows." . . . Socrates: Then anyone who leaves behind him a written manual, and likewise anyone who takes it over from him, on the supposition that such writing will provide something reliable and permanent, must be exceedingly simple-

> minded; . . . if he imagines that written words can do anything more than remind one who knows that which the writing is concerned with.

Here Plato describes writing as a scary phenomenon that may well be robbing us from a much richer experience of life. Consider the traditional stories that elders told you before you learned to read. Good chance you can repeat them verbatim beginning with, "Once upon a time . . . " Now consider a piece closer to you in time, for example, Chapter 3 of your second grade reading book. Try to repeat that story verbatim. Can't do it? Gee, maybe it's because you read it. Having material in print allows you to save it on paper or thumb drive or in a cloud and not in gray matter. No great work was lost to flood or fire; anything lost was lost to leaving the cultural memory—that is, was lost to print.

So what do we do with oral history: Appalachian tales, Native American stories, Homer's *Iliad* and *Odyssey*? In the old days, people put full ethical systems, virtual law libraries, into their memories. What we now denigrate as "old wives' tales" hold certain truths of how to live life. When we write down what has been in the oral collective consciousness, we do even more damage than giving ourselves permission and a physical means to destroy cultural wealth. When one person writes down a story told by various zillions of people through various zillions of changing circumstances, all those zillion variants become distilled into the political-social-gender-ethnic-economic-historical-theological-etc. agenda of just one random person: the writer. Writing causes the wealth of oral "literacy" first to transform into a lie and then to die. Despite the unfortunate connection between writing and memory, the idea here is not so much to diminish the power of writing, but to celebrate the power of memory.

EXERCISE

Search your life for discourse you want as part of your self. Put it into your memory.

Back to the ancient controversy of whether memory constitutes a "gift" or a power "learned." The ancient dialectic either-or sort of mentality seems to have had some difficulty characterizing one thing (here memory) at once as two things (here "gift" and "learned"). Considering memory as a gift, we can feel fortunate. Considering memory as a learnable power, we can learn to use it.

    The ancients learned to train, use, and expand their memories through association. Eighteenth-century Scottish philosopher, theologian, rhetorician, George Campbell would later refer to this psychological principle, as "association psychology." The mind has within it certain things. We remember new things by associating the new things with the old things in mind that already exist. For example, if the stuff in your mind or memory looks like:

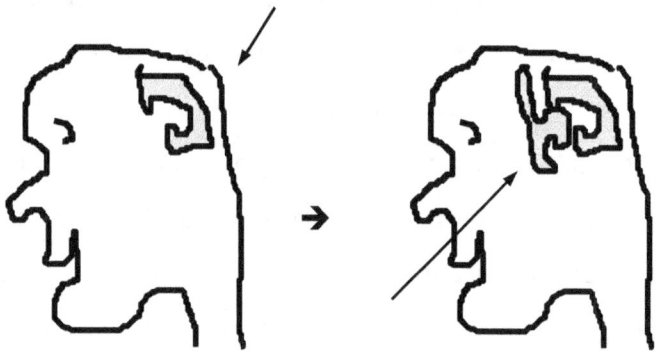

And you want to remember some new thing, then you have to mold this new thing into a shape that will fit jigsaw-puzzle-like into the shape of your existing ideas.

This principle is illustrated by certain software products that "jig-saw" or "interface" into the existent memory of other products.

The ancients taught that a person could plug new material into the old material of the mind by first determining "places" already existing in the mind: some physical place very well known to a person, for example, one's knowledge of the one's own house. "In the first place," "in the second place," and so on would then correspond to the "place" of walls or furniture. In trying to remember a list of proofs, then, a person associated the first proof with the place of a familiar chair, the next proof with the table next to the chair, the third proof with the lamp on the table next to the chair, etc. In a like manner, a running buddy of mine remembers the numbers of her laps around the track (keeping track?) by associating each of the four laps in a mile with one of her four sisters: this is Nan's lap; this is Jane's lap; etc. Or likewise using the principle of association, a literature student once brought to class a different snack to nibble on for each author we discussed: crab salad for T.S. Eliot, kiwis for Dorothy Parker, strawberries for Langston Hughes,[2] etc. On the day of the final exam, this student brought in one piece of each of the different snacks and lined them up across his desk. Popping a taste of each in his mouth, by association, he then recalled each discussion of each author and wrote his exam as the various kinds of snacks disappeared one by one, timed with the time limits of the exam. Interesting concept.

---

[2] Maybe the crab salad reminded this guy of Eliot's "I should have been a pair of ragged claws/ Scuttling across the floors of silent seas"; and Parker's verse certainly reflects the tartness of kiwis; but Hughes and strawberries?

Putting memory as the fourth step to preparing a discourse, Cicero showed that speakers or writers should have a grasp of their materials and words as they sought to deliver them. Customarily, as practice for public speaking, Greek and Roman students put their own works in memory to recite them for others. A bit later classical educator Quintilian felt that students got little out of memorizing their own compositions and had students memorize the recognized "good" speeches of recognized "great" speakers.

Although you probably won't be asked to memorize your essay in your writing class, you might consider expanding your powers of memory to build a store of materials from which you might draw. That is, you might consider memory as a tool of invention. You might also consider the possibility that technology and culture might be nudging us past literacy toward a time when we might value and depend on memory more than we currently do.

Consider what enabled the ancients to memorize those ancient stories. Consider that some contemporary Americans have memorized vast stores of song (especially rap) lyrics. Both ancient and contemporary stories and stores have characteristics that invite memorizing. Analysts call these characteristics "mnemonics," after the Greek goddess of memory and mother of the Muses, Mnemosyne. Rhythm and rhyme certainly help us put language into memory, as does extravagant bragging and remarkable "larger than life" characters and actions. We remember big crazy stories more than the mundane and a little fancy word play can make them ours. As in other non-literate cultures through history, without reading, American kids commonly memorize vast quantities of media lyrics that provide lessons in justice (especially retribution) and visions of desired and undesirable character and activity. Meanwhile, technology moves us closer and closer toward voice-activated computers. Now that we're fairly well adjusted to cars and computers and smart phones telling us what to do, we seem on the brink of talking back. Naturally, using a voice-activated computer will cause us to alter our habits of discourse somewhat. We will have to hold more ideas in our heads as we prepare to speak them and we will have to discontinue our sloppy language: "ugh, like, maybe, like." Student Erin Robinson described using a voice-activated computer: "You might have some difficulty. You'd have to learn to think before you talk."

Compared to "hard copy," organic memory usually proves the more reliable of storage systems. Only seemingly elusive, memory lives in our bodily cells and can regenerate when we reproduce and impart our memory to offspring. Country folk know that the organic memory system provided by plants proves far more stable than anything that humans can create with wood or stone. Spring-time hikes through the woods often reveal perimeters of daffodils indicating where old homesteads had been. With the human efforts of hand-hewn cabins long ago rotted and stone cellars long ago fallen in and overgrown, only the regenerating seeds and bulbs remind us of our history. In a like manner, many of our innate or inexplicable perceptions come from the language we are born into. Such is the strength of collective cultural memory and the regenerative powers of our various traditional stories—don't forget.

© alex74/Shutterstock.com

VII

Delivery

Or

Unraveling the Mysteries of MLA, APA, etc.

As Demosthenes told his pupils, the first three elements in rhetoric are "Delivery, Delivery and Delivery."

"For many poor speakers have often reaped the rewards of eloquence
because of a dignified delivery,
and many eloquent men have been considered poor speakers
because of an awkward delivery.
Demosthenes was right, therefore, in considering delivery
to be the first, second, and third in importance."

—Cicero, *Orator*. XVII. 56.

Legend has it that poor ol' Demosthenes should know. Much like now, back in the heyday of Greece, public attention to soldier-athletes made them well-rewarded "stars."[1] Demosthenes grew up with expectations and dreams of contributing to the

---

[1] Not much has changed in more than two millennia. Madonna has observed, "If I were the president . . . you know, like in some parallel universe where there wasn't any pain or prejudice, where the *National Enquirer* did not exist and women were allowed to empower themselves without being labeled heretical and perverse, then: #1—Schoolteachers would be paid more than movie stars or basketball players." Perhaps the greatest factor determining the relative value to our culture of movie stars/basketball players and schoolteachers is, precisely, delivery. Or as Marshall McLuhan put it in 1951, "Today it is not the classroom nor the classics which are the repositories of models of eloquence, but the ad agencies."

public life of his city state. Coming of age, however, he found that greedy guardians had squandered his patrimony; compounding that unfairness, when he first spoke in the Athenian Assembly, he was laughed at—perhaps because of his awkwardness and "weak voice, clumsy movements, sloppy diction, a lateral lisp, shortness of breath, and a tendency to compose long sentences."[2] Tackling these obstacles to a full life participating in civic affairs, he got a professional actor/trainer to help him develop his voice and physical presence: that is, his delivery. He overcame his lisp by exercising his diction with pebbles in his mouth; he projected his voice by shouting speeches at the seashore against the crashing surf; he strengthened his breath by reciting orations while running himself into exhaustion; he forced himself into isolated study by shaving half his head so he could not squander time and energy fooling around in public.[3] Demosthenes knew the score.

Cicero's reference to Demosthenes should seem especially relevant to us. In our current era, the powerful "voice" of delivery has just about usurped the power of communication from words. In fine dining, restaurateurs know that "presentation is everything." Real estate traders know the profit of the "fixer-upper" rests on physical appearances. Corporate types know well their self-congratulatory communication system of "dressing for success." Rather than legal or humanitarian scholars, we elect Hollywood actors to be our mayors, governors, and president:

> "From now on, I think it is safe to predict, neither the Democratic nor the Republican Party will ever nominate for President a candidate without good looks, stage presence, theatrical delivery, and a sense of timing."
>
> —James Thurber, speaking of the Kennedy-Nixon television debates

---

[2] As described by James L. Golden, Goodwin F. Berquist, and William E. Coleman in *The Rhetoric of Western Thought*.

[3] Since shaving half a head would no longer deter a student from socializing, I suggest just attaching one's leg to the study chair with a simple snowboarding safety leash.

The power of the poseur (or more recently, simply "the poser") has a long history. Cicero portrays delivery growing out of memory—a writer's grip of language and material—that had, in turn, grown out of an arrangement appropriate to subject and to audience and to purpose, that had, in turn, grown out of invention—thoroughly knowing one's subject. Historically, as science and inductive logic gained popularity as way of knowing, they sort of took over the realms of invention and arrangement. Again, scholars figured that they best figured things out and arranged their findings by "the scientific method." Memory often got shuttled off to print, leaving style and delivery as the whole of rhetoric. Thinking of rhetoric as just style and delivery in the eighteenth century began to slide rhetoric into its bad name as a bunch of dirty tricks. Interestingly, a group calling themselves "elocutionists," however, tried to "rescue" style and especially delivery by making them "scientific" too. So elocution became the science of delivery.

As a science, delivery gained tremendous popularity in the eighteenth century. Scholarly research produced books of complicated arm, hand, finger, and foot patterns that could have used line dancing as a prerequisite. Weight, position, movement, and gesture carried ideas and word sounds to extravagant heights. As you might guess from observing disputes in barnyards or barrooms, one puts one's weight forward while expressing one's own position[4] and puts one's weight back while expressing an opposing idea.

---

[4] Note the literal, physicalness of the very idea of having a "position."

For example:
- ☜ Weight back: I see you gave me a "C" on that last essay.
- ☜ Weight back: Clearly, as a poor overworked and underpaid brilliant professor, you made a little mistake.
- ☞ Weight forward: If you had more time to put into each essay, you could see that this fine essay easily earned an "A."
- ☞ Weight forward: On the one hand, blah, blah,
- ☞ Weight forward: On the other hand, blah, blah,
- ☜ Weight back: Now in case you have a problem with blah, blah,
- ☞ Weight forward: But as a reasonable professor, blah, blah.

Unfortunately (in terms of Plato's basing all rhetoric study on the good of the community), some historical figures have used the principles of delivery to promote personal or misdirected causes (as in the above example). Explaining how delivery has evolved until "the medium *is* the message," McLuhan notes the power of delivery in politics,

> Politics will eventually be replaced by imagery. The politician will be only too happy to abdicate in favor of his image, because the image will be much more powerful than [he or she] could ever be.

Consider, for example, the impact of image and delivery as practiced by Adolf Hitler. The photos below show how Hitler's delivery makes literal what has been called the rhetoric of the closed fist and open palm. Notice that several of these photos communicate aggression by means of a sexually suggestive gesture of the extended right forefinger backed by the left hand being balled up into a fist.

ADOLF HITLER

These photos easily illustrate that delivery has powers beyond merely accompanying discourse; delivery has the power to transcend language itself—the very language that delivery purports to deliver.

Comfortably, we judge "books by their covers," products by their packaging, and people by their appearances. Our economy rests on consumers' comfort in purchasing by the power of a slogan or name or icon. Children learn to "read" the sign of the double arches before they read words. Travelers can, likewise, read such icons in countries where they recognize no other language. Increasingly, we can almost dispense with the substance of ideas altogether and communicate by the delivery of graphics and icons. Delivery can help us communicate visually, but again, heeding Plato's warning to put communitas before self-interest, we should recall that delivery must rest on some substance of ideas, lest we find ourselves delivering nothing but hot air.

Whether fortunately or unfortunately, quite realistically, we can be swayed by mere delivery. Likewise, how you deliver your academic paper will have impact on its readers. Consider what you communicate as you submit it late or on time. Consider its form. Regardless of all the time and effort you put into researching and gathering your materials (invention), carefully organizing those materials into a progression pleasing to your readers (arrangement), writing and re-visioning and editing and re-editing your writing to make your language fit your purpose (style), and generally having a good solid grip on your materials and language (memory),—still, a big ol coffee ring, smell of cheap aftershave, or "non-academic" heading with weird fonts can make all your efforts and brilliant ideas look stupid before anyone even reads your essay. We are impressionistic people full of stereotypes of "good form,"

"lookin' good," and "looks smart," so college writers would do well to face this craziness and learn to play the game of academic delivery formats.

THREE STYLES OF ACADEMIC DELIVERY/DOCUMENTATION

Cicero defines delivery as "the control of voice and body in a manner suitable to the dignity of the subject matter and the style."[5] You can apply this tip to writing essays by editing to match your written voice and tone both to your subject matter and to the realm where your essay is destined. You might, for example, want to make your tone in a paper for a bioethics class differ somewhat from your tone in a paper for a theater class. You can use Cicero's advice to make your (written) discourse suitable for the expected "style" of delivery as well. Academicians generally recognize three "styles" of written delivery: Chicago style, Modern Language Association style (MLA), and American Psychological Association style (APA). Although the MLA and APA styles have greater visibility than the Chicago style, you should be able to recognize Chicago style so that it doesn't throw you when you see it. The Chicago style has two forms: one for the humanities and one for the sciences. Use the Chicago style in humanities classes only if your professor requests it. Usually for humanities classes you should use the MLA style. For classes in the social sciences you should generally use the APA style.

---

[5] *Orator*. I. 9.

THE CHICAGO STYLE

Use the Chicago style in sciences classes—chemistry, biology, ornithology, etc. Chicago style uses footnotes and/or endnotes. You insert a footnote (after commas and periods) and then document the source for your information by creating a foot- or endnote that goes: (1) author, first name first; (2) title of whatever it is; (3) other publication stuff, like book if title is an article or name of newspaper or journal or translator or editor; (4) place and then date of publication; (5) page number or numbers. Naturally, each reference you use will demand one of zillions of variations of this basic order. Encountering some weirdness in a footnote like "Ibid.," or "Op cit.," or "Loc. cit.," tips you off to having found a book or article in Chicago style (where the ideas could be either way outdated or a historically significant find). Chicago (humanities) style still asks you to use "Ibid," which is short for the Latin, *ibidem*, "in the same place" and means your material comes from the same place as the source listed right above. If a writer is getting a lot of material from a single source, you might see (or create, if you writing in Chicago style) a whole long line of "Ibid." references. "Op cit." is short for the Latin *opere citato*, which means "in the work cited" and "Loc. cit." is short for the Latin *loco citato*, which means "in the place cited"—that is,[6] not only in the same work at the last reference listed, but also on the same page. That students in the mid-'60's actually learned to use all these little notations correctly may have something to do with the 60's rebellion against such form-alities.

The science side of the campus likes papers using the Chicago "author-date" style. This is not what it sounds like. Rather, you just put the author and the date of publication of the source in parentheses right in the writing that you are doing. Like,

---

[6] Some more old Latin abbreviations for you: i.e. (from the Latin, *id est*) means "that is." e.g. (from the Latin *emempli gratia*) means "for example."

"Brilliant scholars, Smith and Hawkin explain blah, blah, blah." Notice that this example uses the active voice—nice. This form also inadvertently encourages you to use the passive voice: "It has been found blah, blah, (Smith and Hawkin 1897)," which, as you learned in Chapter 5, is not so nice and poses problems in science writing. With each of these sorts of Chicago styles, you follow your writing with a bibliography. In the Chicago style sense of bibliography, you list the bibliographic information for the references you have used or cited in your paper. In other words you create a "Works Cited" section, but call it a "Bibliography."

THE MODERN LANGUAGE ASSOCIATION (MLA) STYLE

Unless your professor requests otherwise, use the MLA style of delivery for humanities classes—humanities, English, art, etc.. In the MLA style, you name the author of your reference and the page number right in the sentences of your paper. For example, "Famous historian Joe Blow describes how under Holy Roman Emperor Charles V, the Diet of Worms declared Martin Luther an outlaw (326)," —where 326 refers to the page of Blow's book where you found this information. Then your curious reader goes to your "Works Cited" page where (in alphabetical order) you have listed all the information needed to find this page of this book: "Blow, Joe. *All about Worms*. Boston: The Slithering P, 1954." That "P" means "press." The MLA style has a whole bunch of (mandatory) abbreviations, like you write "University of Illinois Press," "U of IL P"— no periods. Again, the variations are endlessly boggling. Rather than try to put all these variations of form into your memory, go get a copy[7] of the *MLA Handbook for Writers of Research Papers*. Or consult an "Online Writing Lab" (OWL) or your own college library internet site. Be sure to get current

---

[7] Look in your college library in the reference section or try the bookstore.

information because all these styles of delivery bend and change with fashion and the forms of what needs documenting. Like how do you document an interview on television in which someone quoted a translation from Chinese, edited by someone on the internet? Do not try to know such things; look it up.

THE AMERICAN PSYCHOLOGICAL ASSOCIATION (APA) STYLE

Use the APA style of delivery for courses in the social sciences—psychology, sociology, anthropology, etc. Like MLA style, APA style refers to a source right in the paper itself, but using the APA style, you put the author's name and the date of the source's publication right into your writing and put the page number of where you found the material back in the Reference List. You can predict that confusion can arise from getting MLA and APA mixed up when you are using a book or continuously paged journal where the page numbers get up to looking like dates, like page 1956. To fend off this confusion, with APA you put abbreviations for pages in your Reference List ("p." for "page" and "pp." for "pages"). MLA does not use these abbreviations for "page/s." So a piece of writing in APA style of delivery might look like: "Famous historian Joe Blow (1989) describes how under Holy Roman Emperor Charles V, the Diet of Worms declared Martin Luther an outlaw"—where 1989 refers to the date of Blow's book where this information occurs. Then in the Reference List, you tell your reader the page on which to find the material. And there are various other differences between MLA and APA styles of delivery, notably the order of the bibliographic information and whether or not some words are capitalized. As you got a copy of *The MLA Handbook* for writing papers for your humanities classes, get a copy of the *Publication Manual of the American Psychological Association* if you have to (get to) use APA style, so that you can look up all the little form requirements and put your work in perfect form for delivery.

DELIVERY: THE HEADING & HINTS

For essays in the humanities, which includes such writing classes as this one, your heading should look like this:

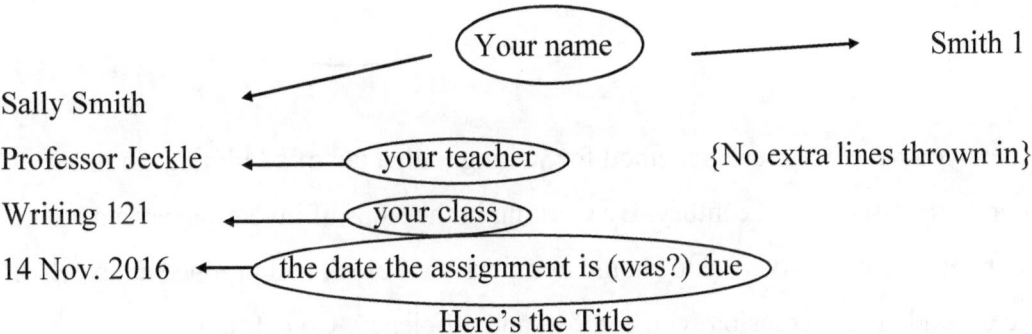

Do not make all this stuff even on the right side (justified). Somewhere readability studies show that eyeballs can hit the correct line better when the lines are all scraggily on the right. Double space. Rather than asking your teacher such potentially embarrassing questions as "Do you have a PhD?" or "Just what gender are you?" just write "Professor So-in-So." Evidently, the MLA considers "Professor" as a vocation rather than a title. Also, write the date in military style, with the day before the month.

On each page put your last name (no comma) and the page number. If you are using MS Word you can accomplish this seemingly simple feat by clicking on "<u>V</u>iew" up there on the toolbar. Then click "<u>H</u>eader and Footer." Then tab over to the right side and type you last name and space and then click the little # button to get the page numbers. If you do not want your last name and page number on the first page (because your name is already over there on the left), then **before** you do the "<u>V</u>iew," "<u>H</u>eader and Footer" thing, on your toolbar, press "<u>I</u>nsert" and then choose "Page N<u>u</u>mbers." In the message box that appears, under alignment choose "right" and get rid of the "<u>X</u>" where it says, "<u>S</u>how Number on First Page." **Then** do the "<u>V</u>iew," "<u>H</u>eader and Footer" thing, without messing with the page number button or you'll end up with two page numbers and much frustration of how to get rid of one.

So there you have it. Cicero's method for writing with a tad of ad libbing[8] to bring you up to the twenty-first century. By working in the steps of invention, arrangement, style, memory, and delivery you should avoid writer's block and produce an excellent piece of academic persuasion with comfort and efficiency. Go get 'em.

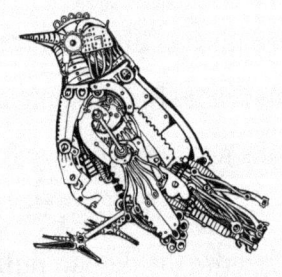

© RYGER/Shutterstock.com 1

---

[8] Short for the Latin *ad libitum*.

VIII

AFTERWORD ~ THE ESSAY

Here's your chance to work using this "step program" approach to writing.

#One: be nice to yourself and give yourself plenty of time.

Work through the various steps here to develop a concern of your own, exploring that concern and gathering information as explained in "Chapter 3 Invention." *After* searching for information, researching, and learning all about your concern/issue, develop some rationale for organizing your materials as explained in "Chapter 4 Arrangement." Then get out the paper towels. Only after gathering your materials and settling on an arrangement pattern should you begin to embed your ideas into writing. Then revise: if you see conceptual holes in your essay, go back and get whatever additional materials you need. Then see if the arrangement needs some fiddling with. Then (keeping in mind all that business about style) edit. Then edit some more and some more. Then remember what you were trying to accomplish and what you have learned of your subject and contemplate your audience learning such things. Then fiddle and edit for style a bit more. Then mess with the delivery format that is appropriate for your class and paper. Whew. And there it is: the brilliantly thought out and researched, perfectly arranged, exquisitely written, well considered, and properly delivered paper!

www.ingramcontent.com/pod-product-compliance
Lightning Source LLC
Chambersburg PA
CBHW080551230426
43663CB00015B/2792